Communication policies in **Costa Rica**

In this series

Communication policies in Ireland
Communication policies in Sweden
Communication policies in Hungary
Communication policies in Yugoslavia
Communication policies in the Federal Republic of Germany
Communication policies in Brazil
Communication policies in Costa Rica

Communication policies in **Costa Rica**

A study carried out by Jaime M. Fonseca

unesco

Published in 1977 by the United Nations Educational,
Scientific and Cultural Organization
7 Place de Fontenoy, 75700 Paris
Printed by S.C. Maison d'Édition, Marcinelle (Belgium)

ISBN 92-3-101348-3
Las Políticas de Comunicación en Costa Rica: 92-3-101348-0

© Unesco 1977
Printed in Belgium

Preface

Communication policies are sets of principles and norms established to guide the behaviour of communication systems. They are shaped over time in the context of society's general approach to communication and to the media. Emanating from political ideologies, the social and economic conditions of the country and the values on which they are based, they strive to relate these to the real needs for and the prospective opportunities of communication.

Communication policies exist in every society, though they may sometimes be latent and disjointed, rather than clearly articulated and harmonized. They may be very general, in the nature of desirable goals and principles, or they may be more specific and practically binding. They may exist or be formulated at many levels. They may be incorporated in the constitution or legislation of a country; in over-all national policies, in the guidelines for individual administrations, in professional codes of ethics as well as in the constitutions and operational rules of particular communication institutions.

The publication of this series of studies has been undertaken as part of the programme adopted by the General Conference of Unesco at its sixteenth session, related to the analysis of communication policies as they exist at the different levels—public, institutional, professional—in selected countries. The aim of the series is to present this information in a manner which can be comparable. Thus an attempt has been made to follow, as far as possible, a fairly similar structural pattern and method of approach which was agreed between the national institutions undertaking the work.

This survey of communication policies in Costa Rica has been carried out by Jaime M. Fonseca at the request of the Costa Rican National Commission for Unesco. The opinions expressed by the author do not necessarily reflect the views of Unesco.

Acknowledgements

The author is indebted to the team of researchers—Graciela Carbonetto, Ricardo Cifuentes and Luis Guenchor—and to Professor Javier Solís, director of the School of Communication Sciences at the University of Costa Rica, as well as to a host of publishers, editors and journalists who gave their views during the survey needed for this study.

The author wishes to acknowledge the valuable contribution given by students and professors at the school in producing a bibliography on journalism in Costa Rica and in presenting an analysis of current challenges during the 1973 Evaluation Seminar. This study includes several surveys made by students.

Special reference should be made to the 1973–74 board of the College of Journalists, under Rolando Angulo, for its support of this work.

Jaime FONSECA
San José

Contents

1 **The concept of communication policies** 9

1.1 Towards a communication policy 9
1.2 Juridical norms 10
1.3 Educational values 11
1.4 The testimony of the communicators 12
1.5 The function of the mass media 14

2 **The system of mass communication in the structure of Costa Rican society** 16

2.1 Historical review 17
2.2 The audience 26
2.3 The mass media 28

3 **Legislation and planning** 30

3.1 The constitution 30
3.2 The Press Law 31
3.3 Laws concerning radio and television 31
3.4 Regulating agencies 32
3.5 Legislation on mass communication enterprises 33
3.6 Laws concerning professionals 33
3.7 Proposals for reform 34
3.8 Official initiative 35
3.9 Other legislation 37
3.10 National planning 38
3.11 The National Development Plan 39

4 **Communication policies** 43

4.1 Methods employed 44
4.2 Advertising agencies 49

4.3 Magazines *50*
4.4 Content analysis *50*
4.5 Comments *57*
4.6 Newspapers and a national crisis *58*
4.7 Media relationships *60*

5   **Professional organizations** *61*

5.1 Present practices *61*
5.2 Society of Journalists *62*
5.3 The School of Mass Communication Sciences *63*
5.4 Other professional tasks *66*

6   **Participation of the public** *68*

6.1 Communicators *69*
6.2 Opinion of secondary school pupils *70*
6.3 University students and the media *71*
6.4 Lack of communication by marginal sectors *75*
6.5 Social solidarity and opinion *78*

7   **Conclusions and trends** *84*

Appendix: Socio-economic and cultural data *87*

1 The concept of communication policies

The concept of 'communication policies' has not been clearly defined in Costa Rica although the elements exist for doing this. The State fixes certain standards for mass communications, the communicators themselves follow certain professional principles and society itself expects a certain type of conduct from them. This study attempts to analyse these elements.

The fabric of mass communications is woven from motivations, standards and values resulting from causes of an organic nature with biological roots. Nevertheless, this constellation functions at the highest ideological level at which it is easier to define the premises for a communication policy.

This study makes use of the juridical norms of the constitution, educational standards concerning human potentialities and the testimony of the communicators themselves. It also reviews the historical development of communications in Costa Rica and analyses contemporary media.

The country is undergoing a process of modernization and is moving away from a patriarchal form of society whose values based on the Judeo-Christian tradition were previously a constant point of reference. These values now seem to be dissolving with their place being taken by new ones of a thoroughly relative nature. Traditions still serve, however, as a factor of moral and civic stabilization for individual as well as social conduct but conflicts of a personal and social kind arise with increasing frequency leading to fluctuating movements of tensions, solutions and indecisions whose common denominator is to be found in conflicting ideologies concerning affluent and marginal societies, although other factors are not excluded.

The conflicts tend to produce survival crises for the dominant system and to require the individual to revise and limit his personal values whether he is one of those in control or an ordinary citizen.

1.1 Towards a communication policy

A crisis has the positive effect of acting as a challenge and a lesson since it defines more sharply than a normal situation the values by which society is guided and puts them to the test. In a crisis, the protagonists' conduct, the criteria orienting the relevant information and the manner in which it is dealt with make clear the premises of the dominant ideology, bring into play incentives and sanctions and reveal priorities in the Costa Rica's scale of value. The banana strike of June 1974 serves as an example (see Chapter 4).

These tensions concerning values and priorities give an impetus to national development and result in some degree of change. When they are resolved through concessions or by the victory or defeat of a given cause, they establish new standards of conduct.

In journalism, all analyses of values show the classical division into appetites and aversions and their categories: affective values of pleasure or gratification with their counterpart in the avoidance of unpleasantness or annoyance; and the values intentionally directed towards the attainment of states, goals or conditions which are desirable as being good. The means for the expression of values can be at the level of the small community or even the individual, at the artistic level, and at the level of the professional commercial media with their large-scale instruments consisting of news, interpretation and advertisements.

There are two obstacles to the definition of a communication policy. One arises from the fact that the empirical study of values is in its infancy in Costa Rica (and even in advanced countries) although various researchers are making important contributions in the fields of economics, anthropology, sociology, psychology and political science. The other obstacle is due to the process of change itself which causes many of the conclusions to be only relative and promotes a variety of criteria as to approaches and priorities.[1]

1.2 Juridical norms

Costa Rica's constitution of 1949 reflects juridical values within the framework of a republican democracy, specifies ideals for the conduct of the community and the individual, and opens up possibilities for the play of adjustment between the interests of the various sectors.

So far as concerns communications, the following principles are applied:
The right and the responsibility of the citizen to express his opinions freely. There is an exception prohibiting the use of religious themes in political propaganda (Article 28).
The right of the citizen to obtain information concerning matters of public interest through public or private sources, except for State or professional secrets.
All citizens can make their ideas public without previous censorship.
Protection against insult or calumny, although this was only partially specified in the press law of 1902 which makes the journalist, the enterprise and the direct directors co-responsible. The individual has a right to his privacy.

---

1. Ethel M. Albert, 'The Classification of Values', *American Anthropologist*, 1965 (New Series 58: 221).

These principles presuppose that sovereignty is vested in the people since it implies the inherent right and duty to guide and supervise the actions of its legislators and officials with a view to the common good. However, the question of a State communication policy also arises, ranging from the possibility of a dictatorial censorship to attempts to direct public opinion towards national development objectives.

Up to the present time, the combination of freedom and responsibility in the matter of expression has led the State to abstain from prescribing an official communication policy. In the almost unanimous opinion of those engaged in communication, an attempt of this kind would be an intrusion on the prerogatives of the citizen.

The National Development Plan,[1] while covering almost all aspects of national life, excludes the re-orientation of public opinion towards development work, although the administrators are to a limited extent concerned with public relations.

Recently, high officials have expressed concern at the effects of what they call irresponsible journalism and at the impact of certain radio and television programmes (although they tolerate abuses in the film industry). They have formulated projects for establishing State television and radio broadcasting stations with cultural and political objectives. In addition, directors of the dominant party have set up communication enterprises (press, radio and television) in order to further their political ideas and economic interests with the admitted aid of foreign capital.

1.3 Educational values

Costa Rican society has a strong tradition of formal education for children and young people which, together with the legal structure and the formative effects of the media, contributes to the formation of opinion. A brief evaluation of some of the constant norms of the educational process reveals the following set of values:[2]

The development of the potentialities of which the human being is capable in the search for personal happiness and social welfare.

The training of the citizen as a member of a social body so that he may contribute to the preservation of the State and of the form of government best fitted to attain its social objectives. The constitution, the laws and social conventions are of little use if youth has not been educated in the spirit of true democracy.

---

1. Oficina Nacional de Planificación, 'Oscar Arias', *Plan Nacional de Desarrollo* [National Development Plan], 1974, San José, Costa Rica.
2. Jaime Fonseca, *Educación en Costa Rica, Curso sobre Educación Comparativa* [Education in Costa Rica, Course on Comparative Education], Baltimore, Loyola University, Citas de Educadores Costarricenses [Quotations from Costa Rica Educationalists], 1962.

Recognizing the finiteness of earthly existence, education is directed towards transcendental values (of salvation).

The preparation of the human being for his vocation, state or condition in life, so that he may in general be able to satisfy the demands of integral humanism and in particular so that he may acquire skills or professions which will give him a value on the market for goods and services and enable him to support himself.

Moral education should provide training for the character of children and young people in regard to personal and social virtues so that they may acquire the ability to sacrifice pleasure and convenience on the altar of duty and social solidarity.

Education is an act of love and of respect for the personality of the student as a complete entity at every stage of his development and his intellectual and moral vitality.

1.4 The testimony of the communicators

To the juridical values and educational impulse must be added the manner in which those professionally engaged 'understand' communication, even though this may not always coincide with their practice.

The concept of 'communication policies' hardly exists amongst professionals and educators in communications even in a rudimentary fashion and there are neither studies nor discussions on the subject although some isolated observations have been made.

Amongst active directors an instrumental idea of communication is generally accepted:

Journalism is made responsible for the principal defects of the political, economic and social system in which we live today. However, our profession consists of nothing more than understanding and reporting what we see and we cannot be accused when we are the vehicle for the freedom with which all and sundry may act or speak. In this play of ideas we are sustained by the fact that we are an institution.[1]

Academic circles point to broader characteristics:

The communicator is constantly becoming more important as educator and transmitter of culture not in the sense of erudition but in the sense that the values upon which society is based are transmitted. The first condition is to understand

---

1. Colegio de Periodistas, *Memoria Anual* [Annual Report], 1973. Rolando Angulo, president, San José, Costa Rica.

and know how to discover these values in the people and the second is to possess the techniques for transmitting these values.[1]

In addition, the communicator should be acquainted with the elements making up his society and the causes of its contemporary condition so that he will be able to contribute to changes leading to a society in which all citizens may participate.[2]

For executives in the field of journalism, a policy is determined by the selection of sources. Some point out that the supply of information is heavily dependent upon government sources, above all so far as concerns economic information, to the detriment of private sources and social and cultural activities. Actual practice confirms the dependence upon officialdom of a centralizing character and makes the progress of the economy the measure of national welfare to the exclusion of other sectors.

The same executives add that communications from official sources to a great extent free the State from the need to devise an official communication policy, since the press already serves as public relations agent through the reproduction which is generally passive of *communiqués* and statements by public officials.[3]

This current is counteracted only by the polemics or replies of those who disagree with these *communiqués* and such replies are rarely provided by journalists.

Other communicators are of the opinion that their task is to conform to the 'idiosyncrasy' of Costa Rican society and to act as an echo conveying the actual phenomena without preference or discrimination. They concede, nevertheless, that within the democratic ideology, emphasis should be placed on the 'social, popular or quasi-left character' of the content of the information they provide and this approach does not provoke a sharp reaction from the right because of a certain degree of maturity in the public.[4] Costa Rican society also shows a certain capacity to absorb 'press exaggerations' without believing them, thus placing certain limits on sensationalism.

Similar opinions are held by those in radio broadcasting. According to them, freedom exists as to the criteria for choice and presentation within the framework of certain general principles laid down by the directors. Some radio news broadcasts check and modify official releases so as not to disseminate 'propaganda'[5] and thus really serve the common good. This criterion is adopted by those in charge of televised news broadcasts which have recently made their appearances.

1. Javier Solís, Director of the School of Mass Communication Sciences, University of Costa Rica, Interview in newspaper *La Nación*, 13 June 1974, San José.
2. J. Solís, *Survey on Communication Policies*, San José, Unesco, August 1974.
3. Guido Fernández, Director of *La Nación*, 'Unesco Survey', August 1974.
4. José Ma. Penabad, *La Hora,* San José; Andrés Borrasé, *La Prensa Libre,* San José.
5. Carlos Darío Angulo, radio news broadcast *La Palabra de Costa Rica*; Rolando Angulo, radio news broadcast *Reloj*, San José, 'Unesco Survey', August 1974.

Communicators in the various media agree in pointing out that there are economic pressures concerning some subjects, either from business and enterprises whose publicity is vital for the media or from media owners, with consequent effects on the supply and the slant of the information reaching the public.

So far as the cinema is concerned (with the exclusion of material imported for entertainment) the premise of the Ministry of Culture when it began a programme of co-operation with Unesco was the need to improve the audio-visual message so as to promote awareness and change, above all amongst the masses on the margin of functional illiteracy or lulled by the superficiality of the 'quantum' of information. Its first productions of the documentary type have the express object of 'giving a voice to the silent' (marginal groups) with films taking a critical standpoint on social problems.

1.5 The function of the mass media

The main function of the mass media lies in the impositions of critical principles on the collection, selection and presentation of news and in commenting thereon with a sense of proportion and direction, within the framework of the vital currents of Costa Rican society.

However, when it comes to formulating a communication policy, the absence of well-defined national objectives is an obstacle that has to be overcome as is also the lack of information concerning the 'various publics that make up the national audience'. A leader of opinion states:

Such a policy should mean placing the media in the service of the participation of the popular masses in the management of society after previously informing them and giving them political awareness with the object of achieving that representation in governmental decisions which is required by a democracy.[1]

There exist elements for a consensus regarding national goals and sociopolitical democratization, in addition to the work of the communication sciences in its early stages, all of which will, in the short term, make it possible to define policies. However, a detailed systematization of the essential data is necessary: the morphological study of the principal mass media, and an analysis of their editorial content (news and opinion) and publicity (advertising).

The professional handling of information requires objective criteria which have not been stripped of their sociological content. A mixture of subjective and objective produces the dialectic of social life in its constant

---

1. J. Solís, director of the weekly *Pueblo*, Survey, August 1974, San José.

advance towards the truth. Side by side with social and political development, there is urgent need to achieve an economic democracy which incorporates marginal groups as an active audience.

2 The system of mass communication in the structure of Costa Rican society

Costa Rica is one of the smallest and relatively less-populated countries of the American continent and this, together with the homogeneity of the population, has given it national cohesion and a sense of neighbourliness. All of this is to the advantage of mass communication.

Cohesion has also been favoured by a tradition of pacifism resulting in freedom from internal conflicts and in opposition to militarism, and by the gentleness of the customs of the people and their innate desire for improvement. Although it continues to be an agricultural and stock-raising country, light industry and services have made notable progress in recent decades. Education and progress are the outstanding objectives.

As the outcome of an historical process which determined social, economic, political and cultural values, liberal democracy is the predominant ideology. The media have contributed to this state of affairs and have at the same time benefited from it. At the close of the twentieth century, the system of printed and electronic mass communication which operates in Costa Rica makes use of modern technical advances although it does not employ all the methods and practices of modern journalism.

Internal tensions arising from the alienating impact of cultural cross-currents originating abroad are not lacking. A society which is a mixture of patriarchal agriculture and stock-raising and industrial modernization feels the impact of world-wide inflation, large corporations, and the cost of transferring technology and from this impact media cannot escape since their financing depends upon a consumer market.

As a result of the high level of education and information, most of the population expect standards of welfare and consumption that exceed their real revenue. By making an excessive use of credit (financed for the most part by foreign investments with little State control) the Costa Rican consumer has created production imbalances and internal inflationary factors. It is becoming more difficult for the poor to improve their standard of living, while the middle class is becoming impoverished.

A small high and upper-middle class group finances advertising for real needs and luxury consumption (total advertising costs are estimated at approximately 120 million colones per year, that is to say, approximately $14 million). The information given by the media relates mainly to luxury products and to the immediate satisfaction of needs.

2.1 Historical review

From the point of view of its mass communications, there are four principal stages in the history of Costa Rica: the Spanish colony established in a subtropical isthmus, from 1563 to 1821; the formative years of nationality, from 1821 to 1889; the consolidation of the democratic republic and its economy and social progress, from 1889 to 1940; diversification of production and vigorous social legislation, including the revolution of 1948, from the middle of the century up to the present time.

2.1.1 *Early stages*

The first permanent settlement was established in 1563 under the name of Cartago. Costa Rica was a poor and isolated province of the *capitania* of Guatemala with no more than 600 inhabitants, peasants engaged in a hard struggle for subsistence, scattered over small plots producing cereals, sugar and tobacco with some livestock and poultry. Information came from the limited exchanges of cloth, farming instruments and domestic utensils. There were neither large plantations nor European masters dominating large groups of Indian slaves and this was an important factor for the future democracy.

It was only at the beginning of the nineteenth century that the cultivation of coffee and tobacco had advanced to the point where their export to London and other markets had become a source of wealth. At that time, officials and peasants became acquainted with the current of opinion in favour of independence which had started in the *capitania* through publications such as *La Gaceta de Guatemala* and, above all, *El Editor Constitucional* and *El Amigo de la Patria*, the latter edited by the learned writer José Cecilio del Valle who was later called upon to draw up the Act of Independence.

When the colonial period ended, Costa Rica had approximately 57,000 inhabitants including Spaniards, half-castes and natives. The country depended upon Guatemala and its neighbour Nicaragua for education, laws and information.

2.1.2 *Formative years*

The news that independence had been proclaimed on 15 September 1821 in Guatemala took three weeks to reach Cartago over difficult routes. The settlers took three more weeks to exchange impressions and obtain confirmation before adopting the proclamation. They were suspicious and shrewd people who feared the hegemony of Guatemala and limitations to the *de facto* freedom which they enjoyed because of their isolation.

Knowing that they were self-sufficient, they accepted basic ideas for structuring their new nationality. One of these was the press law of May 1832:

Freedom of thought and communication consists of the ability to express an opinion and criticize those holding power. Freedom of thought is so absolute that it cannot be limited.[1]

There then appeared a politically orientated journalism which attempted to educate a sparse and unruly population in republican life as an autonomous nation and to free it from the residues of colonialism. The struggle for political power which began a little later clearly defined two groups: those in favour of a rapid change and the cautions defenders of a slow transition.

The writings in which they state their case defend the ideology of French liberalism, which they only partly understood. The first channel of communication was the assembly of notables of the neighbourhood, following the pattern of the assemblies of the eighteenth century in France. They discussed writings, proclamations, books and the scanty news brought to them from abroad by an inefficient press. From these assemblies arose the first *juntas de gobierno* consisting of lawyers, merchants and priests and their objectives were elections, private property, representation of the citizen body and progress.

With the arrival of the printing press, these élites developed a journalism devoted to the expression of opinion and to political education in the service of peasant owners. The Spanish monopolies or *estancos* relating to tobacco and other products having been broken up, coffee and sugar plantations prospered freely. The *pacto de concordia* proclaimed by the first government in 1821 stated:

Costa Rica has absolute freedom and exclusive possession of its rights to constitute for itself a new form of government. . . . The province recognizes and respects civil liberty, property and the other natural and legitimate rights of every person and of all peoples or nations.

Amongst the first decrees published by Juan Mora Fernández, the first head of State, and the Constituent Congress, was the following, intended to promote the production of newspapers:

The citizens are invited to establish in each township of the State a public periodical paper which shall publish such writing as are sent to it.

The preamble of the law stated: 'that the principal basis for a free government is enlightenment which can be advanced by the publication of manuscript periodicals . . .'.

From 1824 to 1834 manuscript periodicals such as *La Tertúlia Patriótica, El Correo de Costa Rica, El Noticioso Universal* and later *La Tertúlia* did in fact appear. With the arrival of the first printing press in 1830, brought

---

1. Antonio Zelaya, *Cien Años de Libertad de Prensa en Costa Rica* [A Hundred Years of Press Freedom in Costa Rica], San José, Costa Rica, 1925.

in by the Costa Rican Miguel Carranza, some began to be printed. An editorial which *El Noticioso Universal* published in 1833 is revealing:

> Under this title we propose to publish a weekly newspaper which will contain all the news which we can gather and which can be considered as possessing interest and influence for the good of society; whether such news is political, statistical, historical, economic or of any other type. We shall also edit and reproduce extracts which may for any reason seem useful to us from writings which have come into our hands but which could not be published in any other way. We shall publish legislative resolutions and the decisions, provisions and official documents of the other powers which it may seem desirable to make known to the public and we shall make such observations as are within our limited powers as to the advantages or disadvantages they possess from the standpoint of the interests of the State and the principles of the régime which has been established.

It promised to publish news judged to be for the public good and editorial interpretations on various subjects such as the policies of the public powers with comments concerning their 'advantages or disadvantages' for the national community.

La Tertúlia, published by Father Vicente Castro, known as 'Father Arista' because of his energetic advocacy of advanced liberalism, had such an impact that it brought down a government by accusing it of negligence and inefficiency.

Following a military government and the restoration of a civilian régime which culminated in the establishment of a liberal constitution in 1844, José Maria Castro, a lawyer educated at the University of León (Nicaragua), came to power and with his friends published *El Mentor Costarricense* in order to disseminate their democratic ideas. His ideas were as follows:

> Freedom of the press is a right guaranteed by law and as such must be respected whatever consequences of its exercise may follow for me. . . . That is why we are the educators, rather than the representatives, of a people which has only recently emerged from infancy. . . .
> Freedom without enlightenment or knowledge seems to be an absurdity.

Towards the middle of the nineteenth century publications began to appear which dealt with matters of every-day life or were humorous in style or devoted to political satire, such as *El Guerillero*. At that time there existed twenty-one small hand-made presses which printed slowly from wooden plates. Some published official documents while others were independent. Editions varied from 500 to 600 copies. The population was approaching 60,000 and was 42 per cent literate.

The policies of other nations had only a limited effect on the country until after the middle of the century; but in 1856 the war against the slave-dealers from the south of the United States, commanded by William Walker, took place and this war had the double effect of consolidating the sense of nationality and strengthening the popular democratic feeling. The war also raised the question of the value of the Central American isthmus for inter-ocean traffic and the fact that it was won by the Central Americans contributed to the victory of the north in the United States.

However, the most important contribution was that made to international law, since the war against the filibusters alerted America to the expansion towards it of the European colonial powers, particularly England, and limited the development of the dangerous Southern ideology of *manifest destiny* which nurtured unhealthy imperialism in the United States.[1]

In order to attract combatants, Walker published in his newspaper *El Nicaraguense* tempting invitations to armed immigrants, including promises of land and monetary benefits, and had them reproduced in southern newspapers in the United States. He also asserted the right to liberate and civilize a nation, Nicaragua, which was divided by local conflicts ('manifest destiny').

The newspapers of Guatemala, El Salvador, Honduras and Costa Rica alerted opinion to the invasion of Central American sovereignty by the filibusters. The President of Costa Rica, Juan Raphael Mora, published his proclamation in the press against 'a gang of foreigners, the scum of all the nations' which was preparing to invade Costa Rica after having taken control of Nicaragua and promised: 'We are not going to fight for a scrap of land nor ... for sacrilegious parties. We are going to fight to free our brothers from the most iniquitous tyranny.'

Mora sent emissaries to Washington in order that, with the support of the press, they could open the eyes of politicians in the United States to the dangerous consequences of Walker's enterprise, which was an attempt to dominate the interocean route passing through the San Juan river and Lake Managua. The war was won in 1857.

Much effort was however necessary for the country to heal its wounds, overcome the effects of an epidemic and reconstruct its economy. Several years later Dr José María Castro was re-elected into power and freedom of opinion was then restored, the schools were improved, the network of communications was extended and the first telegraph lines were established between Cartago and the port of Puntarenas on the Pacific.

On one occasion the lines were cut by those who said they were 'the Devil's wires'.

Following the adoption of a new constitution and the revival of civic spirit, the national goals were education and material progress. The government engaged many well-known European professors who not only taught but also wrote and contributed to newspapers.

---

1. Jaime Fonseca, *La Guerra Civil—Campana Centroamericana Contra los Filibusteros* [The Civil War—the Central American Campaign against the Filibusters], Organization of Central American States, San Salvador, El Salvador, 1956.

The task faced by the mass media was to strengthen the elective process. During almost fifty years of republican life, elections had been the result of meetings of clubs and of negotiations amongst the landholding élites, the wealthiest of whom were coffee planters and exporters, while some, although very few, elections were imposed by military force.

However, as its resources increased, Costa Rica was rising above the village level and was aspiring to become a nation. The coffee crop rose from 500 *quintales* in 1832 to more than 20 million kilograms in the final decades of the nineteenth century. The export of agricultural products enriched a group of 'powerful' families which began to monopolize land and business enterprises, to import machinery in order to improve production and to modernize the regions in which they lived. Taxes provided the government with additional resources for public works, education and health services.

External credit grew as London, Hamburg and other coffee-trading centres made advances on future crop production. During this period the number of small agricultural landowners diminished, and many of them became landless peasants working as labourers for a coffee or sugar producer. The coffee processing plant and the sugar refinery or mill became centres of rural influence although other activities and crafts also prospered. With economic hegemony came political hegemony, and the peasants' vote was controlled by the landlords.

The task of the writer was to struggle for change. The hegemony of the coffee growers suffered a reverse with the dictatorship, which lasted for almost ten years (1872–80), of General Tomás Guardia whose political ability enabled him to remove this élite from power and he even managed to exile some of its leaders. He gradually destroyed the influence of the military, a heritage of the war against the filibusters, and substituted his own firmness for it. In addition, he extended the railway and road systems and added the cultivation of the banana to that of the two other principal export products.

Under his dictatorship, the press suffered restrictions, but two intellectual centres came into being, the Universidad de Santo Tomás and the Colegio de San Luis Gonzaga where generations were trained, inspired with republican ideas, progressive doctrines and scientific culture, and all this was furthered by the increasing trade with Europe.

This progress and the development of public education towards the end of the 1880s stimulated journalism which transmitted more information on subjects more closely linked to national goals. The promotion of political ideas at the popular level was evident and little by little the peasant freed himself from electoral subjection to the landlord. After the end of Guardia's dictatorship, Congress and the press assumed the task of restoring civil liberties and promoted science and progress. The historian Carlos Monge sums up as follows:

In this way the nation moves from the patriarchal to the liberal stage and leadership passes from the families of coffee plantation owners to intellectuals who write for the newspapers. Parties arise which, rather than representing ideologies (conservatives or liberals), are groups of individuals formed around their leaders, illustrious citizens, with virtues and defects which the people recognize. But they nevertheless place this faith in their writings and speeches, provided they know how to strike the right note. ....[1]

2.1.3 Consolidation of democracy

A conflict between party personalities concerning the honesty of the elections culminated in the popular revolution of 1889, in which women participated. The opposition press, which already functioned on the basis of a broad platform of popular political consciousness, accused the government of dishonesty in the elections and cited specific cases of attacks on groups of electors by the police and government officials.[2]

The two preceding decades had seen the newspaper associated with meetings of élitist clubs superseded by commercial enterprises based on readership and advertisers, such as *El Telégrafo* (1875) and *La Gaceta* (1878) which are dailies, unlike the twittering weeklies of the earlier period.

In 1877, *La República* showed the strength of the independence which the press had acquired at that time when it criticized the dictator Guardia for the high cost of the railway to the Atlantic. *La Chirimía* gave 33 per cent of its space to politics and 14 per cent to literature, with 22 per cent for history and social events and the rest for information and advertising. (On the other hand, *El Guerillero* in its day gave approximately 73 per cent of its space to politics and approximately 24 per cent to literature.) The *Diario de Costa Rica* (1885) had a skilfully arranged business and editorial structure and was well written and presented, with up-to-date national and international news, columns of comment and, during electoral campaigns, a good ration of politics.

During the same period, *La Prensa Libre* appeared in opposition to the government.

In his study, Carlos Morales attributes to political polemics the appearance of various publications (*La República* and *La Prensa Libre* amongst others) which oscillate between informational and political journalism and concludes:

It is worth noting that experience shows that all newspapers which adopt combative political lines end by their readers losing faith in them (credibility) and by being closed down either by the government or by their creditors.

---

1. Carlos Monge Alfaro, *Historia de Costa Rica* [History of Costa Rica], rev. ed., Editorial Trejos, San José, Costa Rica, 1974.
2. Carlos Morales, *Diarios Costarricenses Nacen y Mueren a la Sombra de la Politica* [Costa Rican Newspapers are Born and Die in the Shadow of Politics]. University of Costa Rica, School of Journalism, 1971. (Degree thesis.) San José, Costa Rica.

There was another dictatorship from 1890 to 1894 which this time bore the characteristics of a religious conflict centred round two newspapers, *Eco Católico* and *La Uníon Católica* and the Union Católica party, which claimed that it was fighting against the anticlericalism of the generation educated at Santo Tomás and the San Luis Gonzaga secondary school. That generation held that the power of the Church was directed towards limiting the social mobility necessary for progress.

The dictatorship closed several newspapers, a journalist was arrested because of his professional activities and the Congress censured the government. The court of justice upheld an appeal under *habeas corpus* lodged by the journalist and this exacerbated the conflict with the dictator. When, in a pastoral letter, the bishop reiterated the doctrine of Leo XIII concerning the just wages of day-labourers and craftsmen and condemned certain abuses of capitalism, the government dissolved the party.

The effects were prolonged in the heat of political passions and a style of polemic involving insult and calumny. The restrictive press law came into being in this climate.

Towards the end of the century the country had more than 282,000 inhabitants whose literacy reflected the growth of the educational system. Coffee, bananas and other products financed a good postal and telegraph system in addition to railways, roads and schools. The popular revolt of 1889 had the support of a more conscious public than the war of 1856 and the electoral process was becoming stronger.

The country had transformed itself into a commercial centre the like of which was rare in Latin America, with good European markets and credit based on the gold standard. Since there was trade, there was advertising, and the resources therefrom enabled newspapers to become self-sufficient and to bring a popular message to a mass audience. They subscribed to cable services and acquired teletype and Linotype machines and rotary presses. The influence of North American journalism showed itself in the distinction made between information and opinion.

The press was on the threshold of the consumer society.

With the coming of the twentieth century, other challenges appeared. Groups of merchants and coffee planters maintained a private monopoly of capital and credit, and when the government attempted to break it up in 1902, a controversy over banking reform began in the press and soon became the subject of the electoral struggle of the period. A journalist, Antonio Zambrana, went from town to town in search of votes in favour of a new government capable of promoting banking and land reform.

In the first decade of the century, the population amounted to nearly 350,000 and there was great progress in the development of infrastructure such as schools, gas and water mains, a network of roads, bridges, lighting facilities, markets and drainage. Trade continued to develop with the export of bananas and coffee as well as cocoa. When, at the end of the First World War, an impoverished administration introduced new taxes on the profits of exporters, the result was a *coup d'état* and another military dictatorship.

Once more a civilian group of lawyers and journalists, the most prominent of whom was Rogelio Fernandez Güell, re-established the alternation of power by electoral means.

The social question then came to the fore once again. The masters of production and capital sought maximum profits at the expense of the workers who constituted the majority, as the historian Carlos Monge stated. This situation, together with a more intense popular consciousness as to social justice, resulted in an era of demands advanced by political reformers who were precursors of the Christian Socialism of the 1940s. The press contributed to the ensuing controversy between the conflicting interests.

The socio-economic pressure of the peasants and workers was resisted by those in power who were aware that satisfaction of the demands made would have to be financed from their profits. From the 1920s onwards, the Reformist Party of the ex-priest Jorge Volio devoted itself to bringing about radical changes in Costa Rican society and this commitment was later inherited by the Communist Party.

Towards 1936, the government carried out a banking reform with the object of stimulating the industrial and agricultural sectors and of creating new sources of employment. In the following decade, the executive power and the Congress introduced social legislation relating to social security, labour regulations, minimum wages and credit for the purpose of promoting co-operatives and the trade union movement.

The reform group, headed by Dr Raphael Angel Calderón Guardia, lost popularity, in spite of its worthy aims, when it attempted to extend its stay in power. Unsupported accusations of corruption together with communist influence gave grounds for repeated attacks by the rich. Of the various opposition groups, the strongest ideologically and structurally proved to be the one led by José Figueres, a farmer opposed to those entrenched in power as well as to the Marxists. In the opinion of several historians, the revolution of 1948 which he led was the most significant political fact of the century.

2.1.4 *Towards economic democracy*

Popular support for the revolution was not the result of a few months of tension. It was a question of the traditional defence of popular suffrage together with pressures due to social demands put forward by the unions, the students, and an élite of reformers (which was later to form the Liberación Nacional Party) and the widespread diffusion of socialism and christian socialist doctrine. The effective leader of this group was the Archbishop of San José, Monsignor Victor Manuel Sanabria.

In the following years, the constitution was revised. Liberal capitalism of the European type was replaced, not without a struggle, by a social democracy with an economic content, based on a far-reaching redistribution of wealth (taxes and subsidies) together with a re-organization of services by various means: State control of bank credit in order to direct it away from luxuries towards production, semi-autonomous institutes for housing, insurance, electricity, gas and water mains, higher education, etc., and the extension of social services. The fundamental objective was the increase of popular participation in production, the improvement of the techniques and the wider diffusion of vital services and the promotion of small businesses.

At the same time, the number of consumers increased, with the consequent strengthening of the internal market, advertising and the mass media which have come to participate actively in the shaping of the new society.

Towards the middle of the century, two morning papers were published, *La Tribuna*, a business paper although supporting Calderón, and the *Diario de Costa Rica* which began a second phase under Otilio Ulate, statesman and journalist. Two evening papers also appeared: *La Hora* which leaned a little towards sensationalism and *La Prensa Libre* which is more a business paper without political ideology.

Figueres' group which launched the Liberación Nacional Party decided also to found *La República* (unconnected with the previous paper of the same name) which, after its decline as the mouthpiece of political opinion was taken over by commercial interests and became an independent daily.

The strongest newspaper organization is that of the daily *La Nación* (1947) founded by a powerful group of businessmen, the Associación Nacional de Federaciones de Empresa (ANFE), which devotes itself to criticism of the process of social reform. It combines resources derived from the advertising of enterprises belonging to the owners with the dividends which the latter receive from their investments and this leads to an indisputable economic hegemony maintained by wide circulation and good management.

There are also organs for specific interests such as *Trabajo* for the Communist Party, *Eco Católico* for the Church, the oecumenical weekly *Pueblo* for social and political criticism and various magazines of a professional type or of interest for the home such as *Mujer y Hogar*.

The provincial press has been weak, perhaps because of the central plateau and its centre of activity—San José.

Although radio broadcasting dates from the 1920s, radio newscasting took shape only after 1950. Today the radio news broadcasts *La Palabra de Costa Rica* and *Radio Reloj* are flourishing, most of those operating them coming from the press or from radio sports reporting. Television news programmes began after 1954 once the strong current of State control which delayed the development of private enterprise had been overcome. Because of the high costs involved, the television stations resorted from the outset to the use of capital and techniques borrowed from the United States. At the present time, both Telenoticias Canal 7 and Abriendo Brecha utilize the same channel.

Editorial Costa Rica has been in existence since 1960, supplementing the work of other publishing houses such as Editorial Trejos and Editorial Lehmann. Most of the titles it publishes are school texts, essays, novels or works on history concerned with national themes.

Today, the media in Costa Rica display a certain degree of technical maturity, economic solidity and a spirit of professional achievement. Some pay the high costs of technological change (modernization of plant and material) by permitting the participation of foreign capital. Another important feature is the power and independence of advertising centralized in commercial agencies.

Modernization includes a closer relationship with the outside world, with its advantages and sacrifices in regard to life style, values and habits of consumption and also in regard to social tensions. Advertising tends to be for luxury products and to extend to over 60 per cent of the space and time available for diffusion. Amongst the media, superficial cinema films and television are the forerunners as instruments for the presentation of situations and values and have a certain 'escapist' character.

2.2 The audience

The occupational and cultural composition of Costa Rican society viewed as a mass media market calls for a series of considerations from the point of view of the historical perspective and current socio-economic studies of the country.

According to 1973 data, Costa Rica has a population of 1.9 million and it is possible that there will be more than 2 million inhabitants by 1980. The number of mass media consumption units (the potential field for newspapers, radio and television) is approximately 360,000 including households, production centres and services. Approximately 60,000 units should be deducted from the potential number since they are in remote or very poor regions.

The economically active population varies between 300,000 and 570,000 depending upon the criteria which are applied. In certain areas work is begun at 12 years of age and in others at 20 years of age. Account should be taken of the fact that 57 per cent of the present population are under 17 years of age.

Of the potentially productive population, there are 200,000 persons usually employed excluding those living on incomes and shareholders in limited companies.

The occupational breakdown is as follows: professionals, technicians and other specialists, 21,000; managers, administrators and other executives, 7,000; office workers and related occupations, 2,500; salesmen and related occupations, 24,000; farmers, stock-breeders and other engaged in fishing, hunting and forestry, 11,000; transport and related occupations, 9,000; craftsmen and those employed in processing, building work, mechanical industries and graphic arts, 40,000; personal services and related occupations, 28,000; unqualified workers and labourerss, 12,000; and unclassified workers, 3,000.

The figures for unemployment also vary, from 10,000 to 25,000, to which must be added the number of underemployed. The number of immigrants together with tourists per year is estimated to be 100,000 and of this number approximately 20,000 may remain permanently in the country.

Incomplete but indicative studies of the economic composition of the mass-communication audience show the following incomes:[1] 2,800 persons earned $82 per week or more; 6,200 earned from $46 to $81 per week; 8,900 earned from $29 to $45 per week; and 17,500 persons earned from $20 to $44 per week. A further 24,500 persons earned from $15 to $43 per week; some 16,700 persons earned from $12 to $14 per week; and 17,500 earned from $9 to $11 per week. Approximately 19,000 had a weekly wage of from $6 to $8 and 5,100 earned from $3 to $5 weekly while approximately 1,400 persons earned less than $3 per week.

These figures show that the first two groups, with a total of 9,000 persons, plus those with private incomes and investments, have the best access to the means of production and can control economic and political decisions. The following two groups totalling approximately 26,400 persons would make up the middle sector and the remaining groups constitute the poor sector with approximately 84,200 persons or roughly 70 per cent of the population.

Other factors influence the distribution of the audience and of the communicators in the mass-communication market. One of these factors is the distribution of each occupational group in the various sectors such as agriculture, manufacturing, building, electricity, trading, transport, services, etc. For example, even though the country is 65 per cent rural and depends on the export of the products of agriculture and stock-breeding for almost 90 per cent of its revenues and foreign exchange, the distribution of those in the better-educated groups does not correspond to these figures.

In fact, only 160 of the professionals and technicians and only 80 of the managers, administrators and other executives are in the agricultural and stock-raising sectors. In these same sectors there are 600 labourers and other qualified workers.

On the other hand, there are more than 18,000 professionals and technicians and 2,500 managers and administrators in the service sector which is urban in character. Manufacturing is the next most attractive sector.

Similarly 50 per cent or more of the economically active population work in the primary sector: agriculture, forestry, hunting, fishing, and mining; 20 per cent in the secondary sector: industry, building, electricity, water and sanitation; approximately 30 per cent are employed in commerce, transport, processing communications and other minor occupations.

Even though, in rural zones, the schools, health services and means of transport and communication are improving, the population in those areas continues to fall (from 47 per cent five years ago to 42 per cent at the present time). On the other hand, the urban population is rising with a

---

1. Marcos A. Baeza Martínez, 'Estudio Socioeconómico (Socio-economic study) for the Instituto Mixto de Ayuda Social (IMAS)', University of Costa Rica, San José, 1974.

resulting increase in the service sector. This is reflected in commercial advertising and a growing demand for luxury goods.

Another factor in the cultural level is measured by the literacy rate (97 per cent in urban districts, 86 per cent in rural areas). However, some sociologists hold that because the ability to read and write is not exercised or is very rarely employed there is, in actual fact, much more illiteracy than these official percentages indicate. Daniel Camacho, in his basic work in this field, *La Dominación Cultural en el Subdesarrollo* (Cultural Domination in Underdevelopment), makes the mass media partly responsible for this state of affairs and this regression which is also documented by other studies.

2.3 The mass media

Figures collected by advertising sources indicate that three morning and two evening daily newspapers have a circulation of between 120,000 and 150,000. Circulation is not certified but *La Nación* is usually given about 35 per cent; *Excelsior*, a new competitor, about 20 per cent; *La República*, about 15 per cent and the rest is attributed to *La Prensa Libre* and *La Hora*. *Pueblo* and *Eco Católico*, both weeklies, claim to have a circulation of 22,000 and more than 10,000 respectively.

There are two other weeklies, which are published in English, for the large North American colonies and others, namely, *Tico Times* and *San José News*.

Of the thirty or more commercial radio broadcasting stations, four have radio newscasts: Radio Reloj, Radio Columbia, Radio Centro and Radio Monumental. A study of their audiences gives the following rating on a scale of 33: Reloj, 5.8; Columbia, 4.2; Centro, 2.7; Monumental, 2.3.

Channel 7 (in which the American Broadcasting Company has invested) and Channel 6 have repeating stations in the provinces. Channels 9 and 11 are being reorganized at the moment at which this study is being completed. There are contradictory opinions as to the merits and defects of their range of material designed to entertain and inform but the accusation of superficiality and alienation (canned programmes) predominates.

Press circulation appears to reach half of the potential 300,000 units. On the other hand, the radio audience seems to be larger and the television audience is growing rapidly. According to cumulative data for a recent five-year period, there are in the country 60,000 transistor radios, 100,000 more powerful radio receivers, 80,000 black-and-white television sets and about 10,000 colour television sets.

There is a considerable number of foreign magazines, most of which have a frivolous content, with circulations larger than those of publications produced in the country. One distributor alone realizes $930,000 per year on foreign magazines and $5,800 on national magazines.

As was said above, approximately $14 million a year is spent on advertising and commercial agencies independent of the media control 90 per cent of it. There are sixteen so-called advertising agencies. When a law for taxing media advertising was being discussed, there were illuminating arguments concerning its objectives, volume, ethical principles and methods of work. The intensity of the competition in this field has forced those responsible to employ modern audio-visual art techniques and to engage in psycho-social research.

3 Legislation and planning

Costa Rica has relatively advanced laws and standards in the field of mass communication although they are sometimes criticized and revised, as were those concerning co-responsibility for offences of public expression.

Except during periods of dictatorship, the State's communication policy was fairly liberal. At times the government attempted to promote public-relations activities as to its work and projects and this tendency is still important.

Concern regarding legislation on mass communication was felt early in the institutional life of Costa Rica as is indicated by the journalist Abelardo Bonilla:

> Neither the birth of the republic nor its organization was the result of the force of arms, nor was its independence. They were the work of lawyers and they came into existence with a character which was at once patriarchal and juridical. . . . The press was introduced and the first newspapers were founded in Mora's second administration whereupon another important factor began to show itself, namely, public opinion. . . .[1]

The laws at present in force cover three main aspects: the content of the message in relation to the community and the individual; the guarantees for the operations of the media as enterprises; and the standards for training and professional practice in the fields of communication.

3.1 The constitution

The Constitution of 1949 establishes the right to communicate ideas and perform acts within the framework of the social community.

No one may be harassed or persecuted for expressing his opinions or for any act which does not infringe the law. Private acts which do not endanger public morality or order and which do not injure third parties do not fall within the

---

1. Abelardo Bonilla, 'El Costarricense y su Actitud Politica' [The Costa Rican and his Political Attitude], *Revista de la Universidad de Costa Rica,* No. 10, November 1954.

competence of the law. Nevertheless, no political propaganda may be engaged in by clergy or laymen in a form invoking religious motives or relying on religious beliefs as a mean (Article 28).

All may communicate their thoughts verbally or in writing and publish them without previous censorship, but they will be responsible for any abuses they commit in the exercise of this right in such cases and in such manner as the law may prescribe (Article 29).

Free access to administrative departments for the purpose of procuring information on subjects of public interest is guaranteed. An exception is made for State secrets (Article 30).

The State shall retain control of electronic services which may not 'be removed definitely from the domain of the State' although they may be exploited by private citizens 'by way of special concessions granted for a limited period' (Article 121).

In addition, Article 71 provides for the suspension of these rights and other guarantees in cases of national emergency.

3.2 The Press Law

The Press Law of 1902, ratified in 1908 and amended by other laws in 1934 and 1944, requires the identification of those responsible for all printed publications and determine responsibilities for offences of insult or slander that are punishable by imprisonment for a period of up to 180 days.

The authors of the publication and the publishers responsible for the periodical, pamphlet or book in which it appeared shall be jointly liable to this penalty.

The same penalty is applicable also to those who 'with their publications attempt in any way to subvert public order or disturb friendly relations with any other country'.

For its part, the penal code requires that, for offences against honour, reparative material shall be published if the offended party so requests.

3.3 Laws concerning radio and television

Radio and television are governed by the Radio Law of 1954 and Regulations of 1956 and there are other regulations of 1958 specifically for television. These activities 'can be carried on solely by Costa Rican citizens or companies of which at least 65 per cent of the capital belongs to Costa Rican citizens'.

Commercial enterprises are defined as 'those devoting themselves to the permanent, lucrative exploitation of commercial propaganda by means of musical, literary, scientific, sports and other programmes of general public interest'. Other stations may operate for official matters, radio-navigation or private services in industry, commerce or agriculture.

The Radio Law established responsibilities similar to those covered by the Press Law:

The owners of wireless stations shall, together with persons utilizing their stations for speaking or transmitting, be jointly and severally responsible for civil reparation for damage caused, in violation of this law or of any other provisions of a penal character, if their responsibility or connivance in the act has been proved. Such responsibility will be of a secondary nature if the punishable act was committed through the imprudence, negligence or fault of the owner.

A 1969 amendment stipulated that the radio and television programmes should contribute to 'raising the country's cultural level' and specified that half an hour per week should be set aside, free of charge, for the Ministry of Public Education and, during the period of elections, for the Supreme Court of Elections.

Legislation also exists providing for the employment of Costa Ricans in the production of radio and television material including advertisements, for which a maximum amount of permissible material from foreign sources is prescribed.

The 1969 law prohibits also the transmission of false news, vulgar language or anything 'contrary to morality' and insults 'prejudicial to personal honour or interests'. It prohibits the illegal retransmission of the programmes of other stations, the disclosure of private correspondence and the communication of information to the enemy in time of war. The Penal Code also makes the owners and directors of enterprises responsible for insults and calumnies disseminated with their knowledge by their stations.

The regulations of 1958 exempt television stations from the radio broadcasting taxes in order to stimulate the development of this 'medium for the free expression of thought'. Some of the programmes are criticized by educationists and fathers of families because they foster 'a sickly sentimentalism' or contain many scenes dealing with crime, violence and unpleasant subjects.

These defects are also common in cinemas, which, however, are not considered strictly as mass media but rather as entertainment and are completely dependent on foreign production.

3.4 Regulating agencies

The Ministry of the Interior administrates the laws and regulations which, in some respects, are in accordance with the Convention of the International Telecommunication Union in Geneva. As regards the material shown, there is a Censorship Department which has a body of inspectors and a tribunal.

Its function is to supervise the observance of legal and moral standards and its field of competence includes magazines and other printed material. It specifically prohibits 'obscene or pornographic texts ... the dissemination of antisocial customs, and the presentation of scenes which may lead to vice, criminality, sexual aberrations and the use of drugs or which are contrary to the country's cultural values'.

In practice, censorship has been the subject of controversy since the social context of many situations changes under the influence of various factors, one of which is the mass media themselves.

Infringements of the mass media laws are dealt with by the regular courts and are punished in accordance with the Penal Code but the Procuraduría General (Public Prosecutor) and the Patronato Nacional de la Infancia (National Society for the Protection of Children) also intervene.

3.5 Legislation on mass communication enterprises

The activity of enterprises in the field of communication is governed by the general law on associations and by the rules applicable to free enterprise and competition. Some leaders in the social and cultural fields propose that there should be legislation defining more precisely the responsibility of enterprises engaged in these fields and these proposals have been repeated by those concerned with communications and by political leaders.

3.6 Laws concerning professionals

In September 1969 the organic law on the Colegio de Periodistas (Association of Journalists) was approved. The requirement for membership is that the applicant must have graduated from or be admitted through the Escuela de Ciencias de la Comunicación (School of Communication Sciences). The member must fulfil the condition that his principal, regular and paid occupation is the exercise of his profession on a daily or periodical publication, a medium for broadcast or televised news or a news agency and that he obtains the principal resources for his subsistence from this occupation.

The law authorizes the temporary practice of journalism by advanced students of the school and by certain specialists such as photographers, on the grounds of financial hardship. The law also admits to the association by assimilation such journalists as had practised the profession during the five years preceding the promulgation of the law. It excludes certain radio journalists, advertising agents and literary authors and this has led to controversies and to proposals for amendment.

The School of Communication Sciences functions within the framework of the statutes of the University of Costa Rica as far as concerns administrative and academic matters.

Finally, the Union of Journalists, organized in accordance with labour legislation, protects the interests of the profession so far as concerns wages, working conditions, contracts and disputes and the observance of rules governing the employment of union members in mass communication enterprises.

3.7 Proposals for reform

Communicators and jurists consider that the legislation on communications should be amended because it is out of date, unbalanced and incomplete.

They point out that complaints against the press go before the higher courts while complaints against radio and television are not covered by the penal code and are dealt with by the municipalities or simply by the police.

They add that the law on insult and calumnies is very ambiguous and covers persons without direct responsibility for the offences. Other aspects of the legislation imposing restrictions concerning the language employed or attacks on the integrity of the State or the individual are not counterbalanced by anything that would stimulate the constructive contribution of the mass media. They also object to the State monopoly concerning radio frequencies and television channels and the ease with which responsible criticism of the conduct of public figures can be deemed to be calumny or insult under the present law.

The Association of Lawyers has proposed that the Press Law should be amended as follows:

For legal and judicial purposes, articles shall not be deemed to be abusive or slanderous which, in their version published by the press or in a book or pamphlet or by radio or television, contain criticisms in which opinions are expressed concerning actions of the government or its representatives or which contain passages which are harsh, sarcastic or severe, but do not contain words which are offensive to human dignity, and in which it is evident that the purpose of the author or authors is to contribute to the improvement of institutions and to uphold democratic ideals of government and that their object is that the officials and employees of the central government or of the institutions of the decentralized system of the administration (the so-called autonomous institutions) should in their actions comply with the democratic spirit and the laws of the republic.

In the same year, 1974, the Law School of the University of Costa Rica sponsored a seminar on freedom of expression which reached conclusions that to a great extent coincide with the criticisms mentioned above and which also drew attention to the dangers to freedom of expression due to economic forces aiming at political or monopolistic domination.

The Association of Lawyers and the Union of Journalists have presented to the Legislative Assembly proposals for amendments, the most important of which is called the Law on the Expression of Ideas. Perhaps the most far-reaching effort in this direction came from the Evaluation Seminar of October 1973 of the School of Communication Sciences in its suggestions for the drafting of a General Law on Mass Communications which are as follows:

The proposed mass communication law should contain the following items:
(a) Access to sources: the right of free investigation or access to administrative departments, branches or offices whose activities are of importance to the community.
(b) A statute for publications: technical and moral specifications for the finished products which are presented to the public; aesthetic, ethical and moral limitations; protection for children and young persons; forms of public co-operation.
(c) Statute for the media: definition of the press, radio, television and cinema (and advertising texts) as means of mass communication; free access of the masses to the knowledge of facts and the means for the expression of opinions; free access of the masses to the taking of decisions with social consequences; definition of the role of communications in development, culture and education.
(d) Statute for the enterprise: freedom of the enterprise freedom of the press, interrelation, special systems. Economic and social aspects of the enterprise, with the social aspect as the preponderant factor. Legal régime specifically for press, radio, television and cinema enterprises. Public control of materials and products. Records. Public and private responsibility of the proprietors of a communication enterprise; parallel systems such as commercial, labour and civil systems.
(e) Professional statute: definition of the professional in communication; functions and requirements; public responsibility; code of ethics for communications. Other activities such as public relations, press *attachés*, correspondents, reporters.

3.8 Official initiative

With a view to reform, the Executive Power submitted to the Assembly in June 1974 a draft law which stated that the mass media 'should be the property of Costa Ricans' or of companies whose capital was completely owned by Costa Ricans, the shareholders being named and the shares registered, in their names.

The action of the president was taken in response to cumulative pressures from professors and professionals opposed to foreign investments in communication enterprises, in particular the investments of the North American financier Robert Vesco. They held that these investments tended to result in political power being exercised through the media.

The newspaper *La Nación*, for example, commented that the patriotic orientation of many media was 'threatened by the presence in the country of foreign capital owned by a person who is the subject of international controversy'. It added that the mass media 'do not deal with material goods or ordinary services but with information and ideas on the basis of which the country orders its conduct and its decisions'.

A little later, the Executive Power replaced its draft by another which did not include the prohibition concerning foreigners. Once again, *La Nación* commented that the new draft made it possible for a limited company with foreign capital to buy shares in communication enterprises. The editorialist wrote that 'The gate closed by the original draft is thrown open by the draft presented at the last minute' and pointed out that 'some pressure must have been brought to bear' to bring about this change. Others expressed their agreement.

At another level, the Ministry of Culture, Youth and Sport is planning a reform affecting television, radio and the press. During the research carried out for this study, the representative of the Ministry, Lic. Carmen Naranjo, stated in June 1974 that it was proposed to make a diagnosis of the output of the media and to initiate a dialogue with those responsible—heads of enterprises and directors—in preparation for a draft law. His statement was as follows:

We are thinking of establishing stricter control over the media for the purposes of defending the public's right to have communications which will be beneficial to it rather than harmful. One of the more negative aspects of the present programming is due to the television serials which, in the opinion of competent people, give a false representation of the expectations of the masses. They are untrue to national life. They create in the minds of young people of the rural sectors to the idea that they will be able to succeed easily in the city, as they do not show the real hardship which can be overcome only by work and study. Another negative aspect is found in programmes dealing with violence, crime and drugs. The North American films bring foreign influences to bear on customs and situations and thus affect the social life and the aspirations of the Costa Ricans.

There is also the task of combating the harmful hypnotic effect of much commercial advertising.

We want to have our own cultural television so that the public may have the means to educate itself if it wishes to do so or otherwise seek entertainment in commercial television.

Legislation concerning the communication media is very incomplete and has thus made it possible for situations such as the present to arise in which there is no control, there are no policies and no responsibility so far as concerns the media and the same is true as regards the advertisers and the sponsors.

The ministry is preparing special legislation based, on general lines, on Unesco documents concerning legislation for the mass media in various countries.

In fact, in April 1975, in the weekly publication *Universidad*, Lic. Naranjo gave the following explanation of the new radio and television law which had just been submitted to the Assembly:

Since the country has no policy governing radio and television, the doors have been left open for an *anti-culture*. The purpose of the new law is to define a policy for cultural and educational orientation of mass media for the benefit of the population.

Of the positive reforms, one is that which makes compulsory changes in televised programmes (for children) since, at the present time, they are given many lessons in violence and crime.

Similarly efforts are being made to increase the presentation of national books, folklore, artists and music which, in contrast with exotic and foreign material, are almost not diffused at all at the present time.

The law proposes the creation of the Consejo Costarricense de Radio y Television (Costa Rican Radio and Television Council) which will be responsible for raising the cultural and educational level and for carrying out research on the impact of these media. The law also reiterates the obligation to give time free of charge for educational programmes, to alternate with transmission of messages by the president and reasserts the power of the State in respect of grants of frequencies and channels.

The draft limits ownership of mass media to Costa Ricans, requires a high proportion of the programmes to consist of national material and establishes control of advertising of pharmaceutical and food products and also alcoholic beverages and concludes: 'Broadcasts should be objective and should not diffuse news or commentaries which are contrary to public order or which impede the course of justice.'

The law announced has provoked controversy in which there has been widespread participation by communicators, political figures and heads of enterprises whose main argument is in defence of freedom of expression, although many recognize that there have been abuses.

3.9 Other legislation

In the commercial field, the managers may obtain tax exemption and other benefits which partly compensate for the growing cost of imported basic material such as newsprint, electronic equipment and spare parts. The law exempts cultural activities from taxes but places burdens on the commercial media.

Another subject that must be considered in this connexion is the situation of labour under the social legislation concerning contracts, wages, working conditions and other aspects of the relations between workers and employers. There are laws prescribing minimum wages for the various occupations, and setting up machinery for consultation and arbitration and labour tribunals for the maintenance of these relations.

There has been little legislation in the international field and the reformers also seem to neglect this aspect. There are few rules concerning the percentage of foreign material in the programmes of the electronic media; another law deals with abuses directed against friendly governments. But concern is only now beginning to be felt regarding the cultural impact of foreign news transmissions and, inversely, regarding the impression of other people and other cultures entertained by the public.

3.10 National planning

Although in intellectual circles there is a desire to agree upon concepts relating to national goals, there are no well-developed views on the planning of communications either amongst professionals in the field or amongst political figures. Planning is reduced to providing for situations in the short term which are ideally desirable as improvements, with 'development' as the ultimate goal to be sought. Some of those in charge of enterprise formulate plans for commercial expansion with a view to maintaining profitable features and covering losses. Communication professionals seek to improve their work and their incomes.

It is therefore necessary to create a consciousness of 'communication for development' in many sectors, so that the collection, selection and presentation of news about national events may clearly support real development values.

An example might be found in information and discussion on a reform of banking, with its impact on the use of credit, the balance of payments and the real purchasing power of the wage-earner. In fact there was a reform in the field of foreign exchange in 1974 which provoked a discussion of this kind in spite of the fact that the officials concerned wished to preserve secrecy. Some of the media treated this material according to journalistic notions of the common good but these approaches fell short of integral development.

Fortunately, concern about the establishment of national development goals is beginning to be shown by many leaders at the professional, university and managerial level. Revealing publications are appearing and there has been a series of declarations in the media which little by little are building up a concept of the firm planning of the process of change wherever it is possible to direct and correct it.

It is the vital role of the media to contribute to a readjustment of traditional values and to the selective acquisition of new values in the face of the following threefold challenge:

In empirical science, that is to say, the attitude of the Costa Rican towards the natural environment and towards natural and human resources; the objective and methodical acquisition of knowledge of the physical and human world in order to channel it in the direction of his welfare from both the collective and the personal point of view.

Technology conceived realistically and in proportion to resources and the state of their real development (rather than an illusory imported image); a technology applied to the sober satisfaction of human needs, in an integral and balanced manner, without excesses for the few and privations for the majority.

Ethics embodied in a constellation of impulses and values directed towards the perfection (excellence) of the individual as a citizen but from the standpoint of the needs of both the local community and the national community.

Some of these postulates arise in the discussion on development and change and on the way to redirect ideas, institutions and means of production, especially at a time when the capitalist system is undergoing a difficult test which, in the view of many analysts, marks its final phase.

3.11 The National Development Plan

The National Development Plan 1974–78, put forward by important members of the Liberación Nacional Party and supported by many production sectors, recognizes that changes must be made through the democratic operation of the free choice of the citizens:[1]

The eminently liberal character of the political system under which we live makes it difficult to formulate and execute development plans with concrete objectives and, for this reason, we need the effective co-ordination of official bodies and the unification of efforts and wills through the broad participation of all sectors of the country. . . . The planning process requires that goals must be accepted by an important part of Costa Rican opinion and for this there must be an intention to initiate a fruitful dialogue with these sectors.

We can confront these problems and make use of the valuable opportunities which present themselves in a rational, coherent and planned way. This implies an effort of organization and a search for a national consensus regarding common objectives. The formulation of these objectives and the determination of the most appropriate ways of attaining them constitute the central theme of the National Development Plan.

The plan mentions the following considerations as being of particular importance for communication tending towards a consensus:

In ten years of sustained growth, the economy has favoured the urban middle-class population without any apparent damage to fundamental values. This is the principal class of consumers of goods and services and it supports the advertising which in turn maintains the media.

This prosperity of the middle class benefits also the groups with higher incomes, but the poor do not improve their condition and this accentuates social and economic inequalities (the affluent society).

A development is very largely due to the increasing influx of foreign capital and this gives rise to serious problems from the point of view of a

---

1. Plan Nacional de Desarrollo (National Development Plan), Oficina de Planificación Nacional (National Planning Bureau), San José, *Diagnosis*, December 1973. Co-ordinator, Lic. Oscar Arias Sánchez.

realistic national dynamism. The planners stress the need for 'programming the role which this capital should play' in development.

The country adopts the consumption habits of richer societies, above all so far as concerns imported luxury goods, to the detriment of national savings. In spite of a policy which results in higher taxes, this consumption continues to grow. The planners attribute this tendency 'to the effect of the example set by the more developed countries which has been heightened by wider and better access to the mass media'.

Foreign investments and the external debt which are constantly growing as a result of the increased consumption of imported goods have progressively led to 'important decisions affecting the country being taken by others' (foreigners).

A tendency towards a reduction in the population is beginning to show itself as a result of a fall in the birth-rate which is due to changes in the composition of age groups and a reduction in the number of marriages, but, above all, to birth control. These changes may be attributed to new cultural standards and family planning programmes[1] which have had their greatest effect on young people.

In the four-year period covered by the plan, it is estimated that 127,000 additional persons will appear on the labour market. As there are already 43,000 unemployed or underemployed, large-scale efforts to absorb them will be necessary.

The plan considers that, in order to overcome these obstacles to development—abuse of credit, uncontrolled invasion of capital, deepening of the gap between classes, consumption demands induced by advertising, and unemployment—it is necessary to reorganize public institutions and 'give the State a new orientation'.

The instruments for motivating the people and the private sector, such as education and the mass media, are not mentioned. Officials of the Oficina de Planificación Nacional (Ofiplan) (National Planning Bureau) maintain contacts with universities and journalists and display posters announcing the existence of the plan in public places, although with limited results.

The communication media, with the exception of a few editorials and articles, have not shown any profound interest in the plan although their readers, the public, have shown themselves capable of adopting a development mystique which they call 'improvement'. In fact, in a growing proportion of the people, consciousness of the privations which the 'affluent society' entails for the majority is awakening and is sustained by such critical publi-

---

1. Luis F. Mayorga and Manuel E. Rovira, *Algunos Resultados sobre Fuentes de Informacion an el Programa de Planificación Familiar* [Some Conclusions on Sources of Information in the Family Planning Programme], Centro de Estudios Sociales y de Poblacion (Centre for Social and Demographic Studies), San José, 1972.

cations as *Pueblo, Libertad* and *Universidad* and intermittently by a few newspapers and radio newscasts.

The plan draws attention to this awakening with the following observation:

The political significance of the social problem previously mentioned should be emphasized. Objectively, social inequality persists and this becomes more keenly felt subjectively as the groups affected become more intensely conscious of it. As society becomes more urban and the educational level rises, access to the mass media increases and so does the gap between the socio-economic strata and it is then observed how the aspirations of the backward groups also mount as they become conscious that their poverty is not only undesirable but unjust.

If the demands of these groups are not satisfied the result could be political instability with serious consequences for an economic system which tends to resist imbalances whether external or internal in view of the guarantee to investors that is offered by a political stability which is a special characteristic of our country.

This recognition of the need to offer stability to investors (particularly foreign ones) is a common feature in arguments about development of the Latin-American continent and it entails a lack of independence in many respects, together with the widening of the social gap, the absence of specifically national goals and the free play of capital in search of maximum profits.

All of this places Costa Rica within the general framework of the conclusions reached by Costa Rican sociologists and by their European and North American colleagues who have studied the mass media that:

- Economists and planners underrate the importance of the mass media in the integral development of a society, as instruments for determining values and attitudes; decision-making centres, in the field of consumption and investment, operate not with a view to the socio-economic and political interests of their own country but with a view to the interests of the country which is the external source of capital and international power. It is the latter country which decides the type, the terms and sometimes the amount of its capital and technology to be transferred and it does so in pursuit of its own objects and interests and not those of the dependent country.
- The mass media depend upon advertising which, in turn, is dependent on selective consumption tending to favour luxury products. In order to expand their market they attempt to saturate all regions of the country even though the material they present in rural and marginal sectors is what appeals to urban middle-class tastes.
- While the mass media support the investor's intention to make the maximum possible profit in a stable climate, they nevertheless, paradoxically, sow the seeds of frustration and discontent since they promote expectations in sectors with scanty resources and appetites, the satisfaction of which is out of their reach or can only be achieved in the very long term.

The plan records progress in the primary and secondary sectors but omits the third sector which is vital to development as it includes education, the media and training in production skills and services, which are three key elements for the mobilization of human resources.

4 Communication policies

The communication media are in the hands of private enterprises and the State does not intervene in the content of the informational, editorial or commercial message except in its supervision of matters subject to legal provisions.

The enterprises maintain very general standards of public service and profitable management. Some communicators hope that the progressive 'professionalization' of the media will lead to the establishment of more precise communication policies.

A recent study points out that the motivations of the managers and communicators have still to be investigated and adds:

> Research relating to various groups of élites, whether they are of trade unionists or students or are political, religious or managerial in character, should be conducted with special care since these groups are decisive for the understanding of the functioning of power structures. Similarly, it is necessary to emphasize the importance of this type of research concerning the new controlling and managerial sectors and their media for the purpose of ascertaining the conducts and the methods of communication they utilize and how they differ from those which were employed by the more traditional sector linked to the old coffee plantation oligarchy.[1]

The study adds that, as the economic development of the country advances, the communication enterprises tend to become limited companies 'being which there are controlled sectors which are agricultural as well as commercial and industrial, some of which have foreign connexions'. The sociologists call this the stage of the consumer society.

Ownership by commercial enterprises does not prevent the media from reflecting popular problems and controversies between the most diverse groups which are often conducted with civic spirit and sometimes involve socialistically tinged ideologies. This is a tacit compromise between the boards of directors and the editorial staff which is generally of popular extraction. Within this pragmatic framework there appear cases of intransigence or censorship in defence of the interests of power groups.

1. Introduction to *Bibliografía Costarricense sobre Estudios de Comunicación Social* [Costa Rican Bibliography on Mass Communication Studies], Escuela de Ciencias de la Comunicación (School of Mass Communication Sciences), University of Costa Rica, San José, October 1973.

In general, there is very considerable popular participation in the media and this has led to the assertion that in Costa Rica newspapers are the work of the people. What could be criticized is the fact that subjects are not followed up for long enough or well enough, in a thoroughgoing way, and that serious subjects are passed over with only superficial treatment.

Two criteria are usually applied in evaluating media policies. The first is the traditional one which considers the media to be vehicles for the dissemination of ideas and information in the service of the majority and positive factors in democratic development and in commerce. The opposition to this view there is that of the intellectuals of the left for whose dialectic the media constitute an instrument of the power of the dominant classes which they manipulate chiefly for their own benefit although there may be secondary effects which are to the common good. According to this criterion greater popular participation is desirable.

Empirical observation, the consultation of communicators and an analysis of the context of the media indicate other pragmatic criteria which might aid in producing a better definition of communication policy.

In the course of the present study, some enterprises were reluctant to reveal their internal policy and invoked the right to privacy and free competition. Those responsible for other enterprises confined themselves to observing that their media acted in accordance with the legislation on commercial association and on the expression of ideas.

Communication presents many and complex aspects which, in turn, affect specific sectors: for example, the salary scale, the composition and aim of the message and the relationship of the editorial department to the advertising department.

Each one of these various aspects calls for a 'policy' in the classical meaning of the term, namely, intelligence applied to the management of a business or activity for the determination of a long-term course of action, chosen from amongst various alternatives, in the light of what is appropriate for the enterprise's goals and ideologies.

4.1 Methods employed

Since 1967, the newspaper *La República* has attempted to establish standards for the various phases of the production process and with some variations other enterprises adopt similar standards. The observations of *La República* may be summarized as follows:

- The newspaper is a product on the information market which satisfies the social need for: (a) the dissemination of news; (b) the illustration and interpretation of news; (c) education and entertainment; and (d) the sale of goods and services.
- The product should possess a certain quality in the form of credibility and up-to-dateness. A lessening of credibility in the news or advertisements reduces their sales and service potential.

The sale of the newspaper for its communication value should produce profits which are a sufficient return for the capital invested, covering the operating costs and yielding dividends and reserves for financing improvements in human resources and in physical plant.

In order to maintain the interest of the public (circulation), which is hungry for news and in need of goods and services, the communicator must know to whom his work is addressed, even if his audience is indefinite and changing. He must give the content and the form a certain quality and must maintain the personality of the newspaper.

News should be separated from opinion and must present background and be in depth. It must deal with genuine subjects drawn from the actual life of the country and with reference to basic values.

A series of interviews with communicators led to these observations:

La Nación (according to Guido Fernández, editor), has been correcting a deformation of the press, namely, its excessive dependence upon information from the public sector (the government) to the detriment of popular and private sources. It now attempts to cover local interests, semi-official organizations and human problems and to publish columns of the popular level.

The emphasis given to notes on economic affairs at the expense of other activities such as culture and social questions is also being corrected. News concerning economic subjects (whether from public or private sources) should not—cannot—be neglected, however, since the press is a vehicle for the play of checks, counter-balances and pressures in the interaction between the State and its citizens. Balanced coverage is a question of the scale of values and the creative imagination of those directing the media.

The editorial staff of the newspaper does not think it shows partiality in the question of social reforms or that it has firmly opposed currents in favour of such reforms, as some have accused it of doing. It recognizes its obligation to ensure the maintenance of the balance of power between the various sectors of production and the action of forces tending towards socialism due, in some cases, to the intervention of the State and in others to the diffusion of socialist propaganda.

La Hora (José María Penabad). Rather than pursuing definite policy, the editors act in accordance with the feelings of the country. In its coverage of subjects, the accent is on views of the left but this does not provoke much reaction from the right, which shows the political maturity of the country. The newspaper serves as a sounding box for the public as well as for representatives of the government.

Newspapers have improved in clarity of exposition and in technique. As regards content, they cannot resort to sensationalism because 'it is almost impossible for the medium to accept it'. The average reader will tolerate some exaggeration by the journalist from a sense of amusement and curiosity, but will not believe it, and this is another sign of the maturity of the public.

Diario de Costa Rica (Julio Suñol). With limited resources the paper has conducted a series of crusades for the integrity of the country, since the journalist enters into an ethical agreement with the community. It is a grave responsibility to mould the minds of thousands of beings for whom news and comments are guides which help them to hammer out their standards for living. It is not possible to inform without educating. This newspaper ceased publication at the beginning of 1974.

La República (Rodrigo Madrigal, editor). Coverage of popular subjects is considered to be fundamental. Its independent editorial policy reflects its motto ('an independent newspaper in the service of the people'). It thus criticizes or praises the government's actions and programmes according to whether they conform to or conflict with criteria based on the common good. It thus avoids falling into the extremes of 'officialism' or 'opposition' or acting in factional interests. It insists on all information and statements being duly documented and proven and on opinions being attributed to responsible persons (attestation). The public must be informed fully and in depth on important subjects. This means giving facts, background and forecasts if possible and ensuring follow-up or continuity as long as the subject continues to be of importance.

La Prensa Libre (Andrès Borrasé, editor). In a democratic environment, each newspaper has its own policy. Information is supplied and, at the same time, attention is given to the education of the masses. There is a tacit agreement between the public and the newspaper to bring to the country messages that contribute to its development. The essential thing is to give information objectively and, to some extent, the guidance necessary for the reader to form his own criteria and his own judgement. This newspaper is not subject to the influence of any pressure group and editorially it approaches the country's important problems realistically so as to help in finding solutions in accordance with the common good rather than that of specific groups.

Diario Excelsior (José Maria Penabad, ex-director of *La Hora*). It does not claim to be an enterprise run for dividends but rather a newspaper working for reform. It seeks to change out-of-date mentalities which are fostered by the 'conservative and backward' spirit of other media. This newspaper stands for the three aspects of social democracy, namely, social justice, economic growth and political liberty. There is no such thing as the so-called communication policy but when one is defined it would be preferable for it to operate at the level of the enterprise rather than at that of the State even although we recognize that the freedom of the enterprise is not always utilized for purposes favouring the majority but rather for the defence of the interests of the few. We prefer democracy even though we suffer from abuses of freedom. (This newspaper appeared at the end of 1974.)

According to those responsible for them, the standards and practices of the electronic media are as follows:

Revista de Prensa (Enrique Garnier, radio). The reading of the morning paper, *La Nación*, as a 'spoken newspaper' for three hours daily with no change in form.

Radio Reloj (Rolando Angulo, director). In order to increase its credibility, this enterprise is separate from the broadcasting stations and its only obligations are those specified by company law. Copywriting is also separate from advertising and a distinction is made between news and editorials so as to ensure the objectivity of the information given. Acceptance of payment from the subject of an article provides grounds for the dismissal of a journalist. 'Oficial' *communiqués* (from the government or others) are verified and statements and sources are checked. The radio news broadcast is struggling to break the *de facto* monopoly granted to the three most powerful media (but does not name them) by certain ministries and other government departments in the matter of access to sources. It collects and edits its own material according to the standards governing radio journalism: the journalists go about in the streets and personally visit the scenes of events. Much use is made of teletype for international news and of the telephone and mobile radio transmitters for national coverage. The objectives of the radio news broadcast are the development of the country, with national coverage including the rural areas. On Sundays, journalists and technicians direct the programmes and, under a co-operative scheme, receive the whole of the income from advertising for that day.

La Palabra de Costa Rica (Carlos Darío Angulo, director). Information is transmitted freely within the content of the legislation under which the enterprise operates and its goals. The journalist applies his own criteria, so far as is consistent with the general objectives prescribed by the directors. It attempts to promote democracy and progress with emphasis on coverage of the 'marginal' or poor classes. Its programme can have as much influence in the country as a teacher in a small town and it should therefore be an agent for change and improvement. There is a professional team of reporters and much public participation. Salaries are 10 per cent higher than the minimum laid down by law.

Television communicators state as follows:

Telenoticias (Mariano Sanz, director). The general principles are defence of the country's democratic life, promotion of private enterprise and the common good, all in a climate of freedom since the State does not exercise direct control. Official *communiqués* are received in a critical spirit although it is worth noting that the official sector is increasing its direct influence in the media by gaining ownership control of various broadcasting stations, two newspapers and one television station. Our journalists select their material without interference from the enterprise, which does however lay down general principles. In general, the managers of the media are responsive to the broad range of interests and endeavour to identify themselves with a wide sector of the public. When they limit their interests to those of their own specific group they must conceal this since the public would not accept them as objective. Our staff are instructed to avoid sensationalism and to stick to sober objectivity. There is extensive public participation in reporting news and in the form of letters.

Abriendo Brecha (Armando Soto Montoya and Carlos Villar). The State's technical control over frequencies does not affect the attitudes of the information media. Official bodies do not even make use of the half-hour per week which the electronic media must by law give for cultural purposes. The television news programme is legally independent of the television station. It is maintained by advertising contracts. Its programmes include national information, foreign cables and in-depth reporting on current events concerning community problems.

The two weeklies with national circulation stated:
Eco Católico (P. Armando Alfaro, editor). Its motto is 'a christian view of the world'. It is a semi-official organ of the hierarchy. Its object is to promote the dissemination of information concerning doctrinal and moral questions and also concerning the country's socio-economic and cultural problems, in the light of the Catholic doctrine.

Pueblo (Professor Javier Solís, editor). It presents itself as 'the newspaper of the majority' as opposed to the media of élite groups and is published by an oecumenical group which receives subsidies from external development organizations in addition to its revenue from advertising and subscriptions. Its journalism is of the crusading type as is shown by the following editorial:

The unalterable line of defence of the people's interests has identified the publication with the workers, peasants, students and intellectuals who have read, committed themselves to the present socio-economic system. Every injustice that has wounded the heart of the country has been denounced vigorously in our pages . . . in the service of that majority which previously had no independent organ of expression to defend it.

The object is to provide information for the wage-earning majority in order to promote their political mobilization and participation in public power. Enterprises of a liberal type cannot bring about this mobilization since they remain silent concerning facts and situations affecting, for example, the trade unions.

The two weeklies directed towards the English-speaking community in Costa Rica and towards tourists, the *Tico Times* and the *San José News*, reproduce the principal subjects presented in the daily press and also have their own columns and comments.

Film production is limited to documentaries and advertising for commercial cinemas. Since 1973, the Ministry of Culture has produced documentaries intended to overcome the lack of communication which is typical of the underdeveloped classes. The motto of the series is 'to give a voice to the silent', and films of social criticism and of a didactic nature are produced.

Various publishing enterprises publish textbooks, essays and studies on history, economics and other subjects as well as novels. Since 1959, Editorial Costa Rica, a semi-autonomous enterprise, has been publishing 'typically' Costa Rican works. Its list contains 200 titles and 40 authors and it encourages work in such fields as literature, science, the arts and biography. It reduces the prices of its publications in order to bring them within the reach of the public.

4.2 Advertising agencies

Commercial advertisements have their own impact on the consumer society and the policies of the mass media but in this field also there has been little or no authoritatives.

More than twenty-four independent agencies are functioning today, some of which are very powerful because of the number of client-accounts they manage and the amount of business involved. There is the Asociación Costarricense de Agencias Publicitarias (ASCAP) (Costa Rican Association of Advertising Agencies) which, with the media and the announcers themselves, has formed the Consejo Nacional de la Publicidad (National Advertising Council). In June 1974, the council adopted the following objectives:

The function of advertising is to supply the consumer with truthful information on products and services. Inaccurate advertising undermines the confidence of the consumer.

Honesty is essential for all parties concerned: announcers, agencies, the media and the public.

Although the principal object is the development of the advertising industry, its managers must contribute to the solution of social problems and aid in development and act in the interests of the whole country.

The agencies operate without requiring from the media certified figures for circulation or audiences. In answer to the inquiry for this study, Alberto Garnier of the advertising agency of the same name stated:

There is no information available concerning the number of copies of newspapers printed or their circulation. We shall take as a guide what the media themselves say. A body for the verification of newspaper circulation does not exist. It has been suggested that this work of verification should be undertaken by the American Bureau of Circulation (ABC) but, with the exception of *La Nación*, they all opposed this proposal or put forward excuses. *La Prensa Libre* supplied us with its figures which were certified by public accountants.

ASCAP periodically carries out studies of the audience of radio stations and television channels, going into some details for the Central Plateau which is the country's communication centre but these are on the basis of 'estimates'.

The advertising agent, Luis Carlos Umana, summarizes his philosophy as follows:

We believe that advertising is the measure for the growth of a country in which there is private enterprise (advertising not being allowed in socialist countries). There are those who say that advertising creates needs, but this is not the case since human beings already have certain needs at birth and these are merely given direction by advertising, together with education, the place in which they live and the size of their income. . . . We do good advertising work while complying with our principles (ethical). We believe that it is a serious profession which is vital to the modern world. . . . We understand that advertising is not a goal, but an instrument. The work of the agency is based on honesty, service, creative genius and reasoning, the consumer deserves the truth.

4.3 Magazines

The majority of the illustrated magazines for popular consumption are imported, and, like the few which are published in the country, usually confine themselves to frivolous subjects, sports and entertainment, although sometimes they give advice or include short stories. Very few of them specialize in professional or productive activities.

One firm of importers reports sales to an annual value of $1 million, although the sale of national magazines does not exceed $58,000. There are in circulation in the country seventy-two comic and strip cartoons, twenty series of publications in instalment and eight magazines concerned with fashions and patterns. One importer estimates that, of the magazines that he distributes, 70 per cent are bought by women, 20 per cent by men and 10 per cent by children. Instalment issues and photo-story magazines are sold mainly in the supermarkets.

4.4 Content analysis

The main contribution to the underlying principles for a communication policy is derived from the analysis of the content of the media. For purpose of comparison, the figures (see Tables 1–4) given cover the same day of four consecutive weeks (May 1974) for the following categories: space given to editorial matter, information and advertising; space for national and foreign news; origin of information by geographical areas; advertising for luxuries or necessities; serious information, trivial information and the respective breakdowns by subjects or categories. There are also comparative tables, data for one weekly and for the electronic media and some comments. The weekly *Universidad* is dealt with in another chapter.

Measurements were in column-inches but shortly afterwards the metric system or column-centimetres was introduced.

TABLE 1. Space given in four daily newspapers for editorial matter and advertising according to edition

Newspaper	Edition				Total column-inches	Percentage
	A	B	C	D		
La Nación						
Editorial matter	2,718	1,811	1,814	1,755	8,098	34
Advertising	3,682	4,269	3,946	3,686	15,583	66
La República						
Editorial matter	1,356	1,263	1,333	1,347	5,234	51
Advertising	1,434	907	1,347	1,308	4,996	49
La Prensa Libre						
Editorial matter	1,480	1,190	1,392	1,539	5,601	62.8
Advertising	760	1,050	848	701	3,358	37.2
Nueva La Hora						
Editorial matter	1,585	1,429	1,575	1,403	5,992	78
Advertising	335	491	345	517	1,688	22

TABLE 2. Newspaper space devoted to national and foreign news and the origin of the latter by geographical area (number of items)

Newspaper	Edition				Total no. of items	Percentage
	A	B	C	D		
La Nación						
National news	79	68	66	70	283	57
Foreign news	*57*	*58*	*50*	*50*	*215*	*43*
Latin America	15	17	11	11	54	25
Central America	13	12	10	21	56	26
United States	13	11	11	3	38	17.6
Western Europe	11	11	13	6	41	19
Eastern Europe	0	1	0	1	2	0.9
Rest of world	5	6	5	8	24	11.5
TOTAL	136	126	116	120	498	
La República						
National news	55	32	30	39	156	64.1
Foreign news	*34*	*22*	*15*	*16*	*87*	*35.9*
Latin America	9	9	4	1	23	26.4
Central America	1	2	—	1	4	4.3
United States	8	4	2	4	18	20.4
Western Europe	10	5	7	7	29	33.2
Eastern Europe	2	—	1	1	4	4.3
Rest of world	4	2	1	2	9	11.4
TOTAL	89	54	45	55	243	
La Prensa Libre						
National news	64	54	44	46	208	68
Foreign news	*21*	*27*	*24*	*26*	*98*	*32*
Latin America	8	8	4	8	28	28.2
Central America	—	—	2	2	4	4.1
United States	3	7	2	3	15	15.2
Western Europe	7	10	11	8	36	36.3
Eastern Europe	1	—	1	1	3	3.1
Rest of world	3	2	4	4	13	13.1
TOTAL	85	81	68	72	306	
Nueva La Hora						
National news	47	42	46	40	175	62
Foreign news	*17*	*21*	*29*	*21*	*88*	*38*
Latin America	7	6	13	6	32	36.5
Central America	2	1	1	—	4	4.5
United States	3	5	2	1	11	12.5
Western Europe	4	7	9	11	31	35
Eastern Europe	—	—	—	0	0	—
Rest of world	1	2	4	9	10	11.5
TOTAL	64	63	75	61	263	

TABLE 3. Content of advertising in four daily newspapers (by column-inches)

Newspaper	Edition				Total	Percentage
	A	B	C	D		
La Nación						
Classified	342	444	406	526	1,718	11.1
Luxuries	2,001	2,773	2,168	1,843	8,765	56
First necessity	164	337	140	322	963	6.3
Institutions	523	294	512	241	1,570	10
Professional services	441	217	395	427	1,480	9.5
Business	211	110	184	114	609	3.9
Politics	0	94	141	243	478	3.2
TOTAL	3,682	4,269	3,946	3,686	15,583	
La República						
Classified	—	—	—	—	—	—
Luxuries	497	465	660	425	2,047	41
First necessity	318	86	62	219	685	13.7
Institutions	337	198	331	559	1,425	28.6
Professional services	—	22	5	4	31	0.6
Business	237	18	62	83	400	8
Politics	45	118	227	18	408	8.1
TOTAL	1,434	907	1,347	1,308	4,996	
La Prensa Libre						
Classified	96.5	131	118	145	490.5	14.2
Luxuries	456.5	569.5	291	342	1,659	49.4
First necessity	—	74	24	70	168	4.9
Institutions	145	200	284	54	683	21
Professional services	17	54	63	65	199	5.9
Business	6	—	45	25	76	2.2
Politics	39	21	23	—	83	2.4
TOTAL	760	1,049.5	848	701	3,358.5	
Nueva La Hora						
Classified	45	45	45	—	135	8.5
Luxuries	148	232	28	306	714	42.2
First necessity	—	160	—	—	160	9.5
Institutions	76	6	100	180	362	21.5
Professional services	38	40	24	15	117	6.6
Business	28	8	148	16	200	11.8
Politics	—	—	—	—	0	—
TOTAL	335	491	345	517	1,688	

TABLE 4. Categories of information in four daily newspapers (all editions)

Newspaper[1]	Serious material							Light material						
	International relations	Politics—administration	Social	Economic	Cultural	Scientific	Total	%	Sport	Crime	Society	Entertainment	Miscellaneous	Recreation	Total	%
La Nación								65								35
News	52	167	40	81	23	9	372		64	49	51	12	6	48	230	
Education	—	—	1	—	12	2	15									
Orientation	5	23	3	5	6	—	42									
TOTAL							429									
La República								60								40
News	37	94	17	32	14	1	195		43	22	26	19	7	28	145	
Education	—	—	—	1	4	—	5									
Orientation	2	7	3	4	3	—	19									
TOTAL							219									
La Prensa Libre								52								48
News	25	82	34	31	13	5	190		64	35	68	6	2	32	207	
Education	—	2	—	—	9	5	16									
Orientation	4	9	—	3	5	—	21									
TOTAL							227									
Nueva La Hora								65								35
News	19	89	22	29	6	3	168		44	30	—	9	6	21	110	
Education	—	—	1	1	1	4	7									
Orientation	5	21	3	4	—	—	33									
TOTAL							208									

1. Data shown are for four editions of each newspaper, in May 1974, one day in each week of the month.

TABLE 5. Breakdown of space in four daily newspapers and one weekly (4 editions)

Newspaper	Total space			News		
	Column-inches	Editorial matter (%)	Advertising (%)	No. of items	National (%)	Foreign (%)
Morning						
La Nación	23,680	34	66	498	57	43
La República	10,230	51	49	243	64	36
Evening						
La Prensa Libre	8,960	63	37	306	68	32
Nueva La Hora	7,680	78	22	263	62	38
Weekly						
Pueblo	6,160	67.2	32.8	90	89	11

TABLE 6. Comparative summary of news sources by geographical area (four daily newspapers and one weekly)

Newspaper	No. of items	Latin America (%)	Central America (%)	United States (%)	Western Europe (%)	Eastern Europe (%)	Rest of world (%)
Morning							
La Nación	215	25	26	17.6	19	0.9	11.5
La República	87	26.4	4.3	20.4	33.2	4.3	11.4
Evening							
La Prensa Libre	98	28.2	4.5	15.2	35.3	3.1	13.5
Nueva La Hora	88	28.5	4.5	12.5	35	—	11.5
Weekly							
Pueblo	10	70	—	10	20	—	—

TABLE 7. Comparative summary of advertising content (four daily newspapers and one weekly)

Newspaper	Total column-inches	Class-ified (%)	Luxuries (%)	First necess-ities (%)	Institu-tions (%)	Pro-fessional services (%)	Business (%)	Politics (%)
Morning								
La Nación	15,583	11.1	56	6.3	10	9.5	3.2	3.2
La República	4,996	—	41	13.7	28.6	0.6	8	8.1
Evening								
La Prensa Libre	3,358	14.2	49.4	4.9	21	5.9	2.2	2.4
Nueva La Hora	1,688	8.5	48.1	9.5	21.5	6.6	11.8	—
Weekly								
Pueblo	2,022	—	28.6	—	62	3	—	6.4

TABLE 8. Comparative summary of categories of information and breakdown of serious information (four daily newspapers and one weekly)

Newspaper	Light (%)	Serious (%)	Serious material in		
			News (%)	Education (%)	Orientation (%)
Morning					
La Nación	35	65	87	3	10
La República	40	60	88	3	9
Evening					
La Prensa Libre	48	52	84	7	9
Nueva La Hora	35	65	81	3	16
Weekly					
Pueblo	16	84	51	18	31

Measurements were also made of time in the case of radio news programmes indicating in percentages the length of time given to news or advertising, the character of the advertisements, the source of news items, when they were received and comments. Television programmes were not measured because of technical difficulties. In another section, the managers themselves describe their format and the aims they seek to achieve.

Radio News Reloj (Radio Reloj) broadcasts two thirty-minute programmes daily at 12 noon and 7 p.m. The two programmes devote 50 per cent of their time to news and 50 per cent to advertising.

Of the time devoted to advertising in the first programme, 75 per cent is devoted to luxuries, 18.2 per cent to first necessities, 3.4 per cent to institutions while 3.4 per cent is devoted to other services. In the second programme, 78.5 per cent of its advertising is devoted to luxuries, 17.2 per cent to first necessities, and 4.3 per cent to other services.

The sources for the news items of the first programme are broken down as follows: 95 per cent is devoted to national news; 5 per cent to foreign news, all coming from Latin America. In the second programme national news constitutes 75 per cent and foreign news 25 per cent. Of the total news 65 per cent comes from Latin America and 35 per cent from Europe.

La Palabra de Costa Rica (Radio Monumental) broadcasts four programmes daily, two for 60 minutes at 6 a.m. and 11.30 a.m. and two for 30 minutes at 7 p.m. and 10.30 p.m. There are also brief news programmes every half-hour for 18 hours. All programmes devote 50 per cent to news and 50 per cent to advertising.

Of the advertising time, 59 per cent is devoted to luxuries, 3.7 per cent to first necessities, 33.6 per cent to institutions while 3.7 per cent is devoted to enterprises-financial.

The source of news is broken down as follows: 82 per cent is devoted to national news, 18 per cent to foreign news. Of the total for news 62.5 per cent comes from Latin America; 12 per cent from Western Europe; 1.5 per cent from the United States of America and 24 per cent from the rest of the world.

The Radio Monumental during the day broadcasts *Breves Noticieros* ('Coca Cola') for five minutes every half-hour with 38 per cent of its time devoted to advertising (luxuries) while 62 per cent is devoted to news. Of the total news broadcasts, 47 per cent comes from national sources; 53 per cent from foreign sources. Of the total for news, 75 per cent comes from Latin America, 12.5 per cent from the United States while 12.5 per cent comes from the rest of the world.

Radio Atenea broadcasts *Comentarios de Actualidad,* or news commentary programmes, with three at 12 noon, 6 p.m. and 10.30 p.m. News takes up 50 per cent of the time while advertising takes up 50 per cent. All news is national. Of the time devoted to advertising, 78 per cent is devoted to luxuries, 11 per cent to first necessities, 5.5 per cent to services while the remainder of 6.5 per cent is devoted to enterprises-financial.

4.5 Comments

According to the data under analysis, of the total of 56,000 column-inches published in the four editions of the four newspapers, approximately 58 per cent consisted of copy, titles, photographs and illustrations, while approximately 42 per cent consisted of advertisements, the proportion being to the advantage of the reader. Revenue from advertising amounted to some $6 million per year on this basis. Advertisements for luxuries in the four editions accounted for 56 per cent of all advertising and classified advertisements and those for first necessities accounted for approximately 30 per cent. Institutions, professional services and politics took up the rest.

In the volume of news, serious material predominates with 60 per cent as against 40 per cent for frivolous material. Of the serious material, communication of information accounts for 80 per cent, educational material for 5 per cent and opinion for 15 per cent.

Of the total of 1,311 items published in the period considered, approximately 63 per cent dealt with national subjects and 37 per cent with international news, coming mainly from Europe and Latin America with a smaller proportion from the United States and the Soviet bloc. The chief agencies were the Associated Press, United Press International, Reuters, Efe and Agence France-Presse.

So far as concerns national information, the coverage of politics and public administration predominates with 432 news items, two educational pieces and sixty commentaries. Next come sports with 215 items, economics with 173 and education with two and there are sixteen editorials or commentaries. Then come society news with 145 items and international relations news with 143 and sixteen editorials. Crime news with 136 items and recreational information with 129 are followed by social conflicts and social questions with 103 items, two educational expositions and nine editorials.

Although the social question has developed acute aspects in Costa Rica, as can be seen in other chapters, the daily newspapers do not reflect this, and only publications of a polemical type (*Pueblo, Universidad, Libertad*) give high priority to this subject. In the sixteen daily editions, there are six pieces per edition with social content.

Culture with fifty-six items, twenty-six educational expositions and fourteen editorials receives better treatment than scientific journalism (although in the field of culture some directors and communicators regret the lack of literary and artistic reviews and criticism).

Following a seminar on this subject (of CIMPEC at the end of 1973 in San José) journalists have given more importance to scientific subjects in the news. The present survey registered eighteen items and eleven expositions, which are low figures for a country in need of technology and of sciences dealing with man and his resources.

4.6 Newspapers and a national crisis

A comparative study of the attitude adopted by the various newspapers in regard to the banana strike in June 1974 furnishes concrete examples of communication policies. The factors which gave this strike the dimensions of a national crisis were the following:

It took place while the government was negotiating with the foreign enterprises which deal in bananas concerning a special tax intended to increase foreign exchange reserves.

For twenty days it interrupted work concerned with the cultivation of the banana which is a difficult fruit to keep and to transport. The industry deals with 60 million clusters per year and accounts for a quarter of the foreign exchange; 28,000 hectares are cultivated.

It directly affected the lives of 20,000 persons and posed serious human problems for workers' families.

The workers asked for better contracts (wages, medical and health care, pensions) and the companies resisted on two fronts: the workers' demands and the taxation imposed by the government. A legal contract which granted privileges to one of the companies was also discussed.

At that time, groups of the left were contending with groups of the centre in local elections in a new administrative unit of the banana growing region.

The strike was declared legal since the majority of the workers had fulfilled the necessary requirements concerning consultation and the Ministry of Labour acted as a simple mediator.

The study covered the duration of the conflict, from 15 June to 8 July. The column-inch measurements include photographs.

Coverage by column-inches

La Nación. Total of general news in twenty-four days: 84,480 inches; news about the strike: 1,449 inches (1.77 per cent of total); 164 inches on first page (10.94 per cent of total); on inner pages 1,335 inches (89.06 per cent of total).

La República. General news for twenty-four days: 59,520 inches; news about the strike, 1,239 inches (2.08 per cent of total); 451 inches on first page (36.40 per cent); on inner pages 788 (63.60 per cent).

La Prensa Libre. General news for twenty days (does not appear on Sundays), 44,800 inches; 658 inches about strike (1.46 per cent); on first page 131 inches (19.90 per cent); on inner pages 527 (80.10 per cent).

Nueva La Hora. General news for twenty days, 38,400 inches; 680 on strike (1.77 per cent); 30 inches on first page (4.41 per cent), 650 inches on inner pages (95,59 per cent).

System of work

Number of reports by special correspondents in the strike zone (Pacífico Sur): *La Nación* 8, *La República* 23, *La Prensa Libre* 0, *Nueva La Hora* 0.

Number of direct interviews with leaders of workers and employers: *La Nación* 13, *La República* 10, *La Prensa Libre* 5, *Nueva La Hora* 6.

Equal prominence given to the three sources: strikers, the company and the government: *La Nación* 3, *La República* 4, *La Prensa Libre* 2, *Nueva La Hora* 0.

Two points of view: *La Nación* 8 (government and company 5, company and workers 3), *La República* 7 (government and company 4, government and workers 2, company and workers 1), *La Prensa Libre* 1 (government and workers), *Nueva La Hora* 1 (government and company).

One point of view: *La Nación* 18 (government 11, company 5, workers 2), *La República* 16 (government 9, company 5, workers 2), *La Prensa Libre* 10 (government 4, company 5, workers 1), *Nueva La Hora* 10 (government 6, company 1, workers 3).

Editorials and commentaries: *La Nación* 5, *La República* 3, *La Prensa Libre* 2, *Nueva La Hora* 4.

Cables from foreign news agencies reproduced in newspapers: *La Nación* 6, *La República* 2, *La Prensa Libre* 0, *Nueva La Hora* 1.

Attitude adopted

La Nación stated several times that the strike was anti-economic. It was of the opinion that the workers were influenced by political considerations and not simply by considerations relating to labour. It urged that the Labour

Code should be amended so as not to support the 'blind' attitudes of the parties. In its news report, it expressed the view that picketing of the plant by the workers was unlawful and harmful.

La República in its editorial policy showed itself very concerned about the effects of the strike and the losses due to it. It criticized the company for not having shown a sense of social justice. The news reports presented the stages of the negotiations soberly and communicated objectively the points of view of the parties and the mediators.

La Prensa Libre gave little editorial attention to the problem but, in a couple of articles, declared itself to be nationalistic in the face of foreign interests. The news reports narrated the progress of the action taken to reach a solution.

Nueva La Hora criticized the company and attacked *La Nación* for asserting that the strike was anti-economic. The news reports emphasized the work of the government mediators and criticized the politicians of the left who were said to be impeding mediation.

4.7 **Media relationships**

Economic motivation is the principal link between the communication enterprises and their associates, as is shown by the Consejo Nacional de Publicidad (National Advertising Council) which unites the Cámara Nacional de Medios (National Chamber of Media) with the Cámara de Anunciantes (Chamber of Announcers) and the Asociación de Agencias de Publicidad (Association of Advertising Agencies). The managers or directors of newspapers and of radio and television stations meet from time to time in order to discuss subjects such as increases in the price of paper or customs measures which may make equipment or spare parts more expensive. Occasionally they discuss subjects relating to national politics or consult one another, on the basis of professional affinities, concerning some common problem, but they do not meet systematically. The competition between the various media is stronger than any possible co-operation, for they compete in expanding their markets, securing more advertising, modernizing production and attracting the most highly skilled personnel.

5 Professional organizations

The policy of the professional groups engaged in communication activities takes the form of going beyond traditional empiricism. Entrepreneurs have been modernizing their equipment and their methods (although at high cost so far as concerns the transfer of technology), and communicators have adopted professional improvement as their goal.

There are some 200 persons who work as professional journalists and they are backed by an additional 800 technicians and assistants. Approximately sixty of the communicators completed their secondary school education (*bachillerato*) and forty of them gained university degrees, although not necessarily in journalism. The rest have incomplete academic education but have educated themselves in the course of their daily work as journalists, with resulting differences in their approach and technique. Only five took advantage of a training course offered by the University of Costa Rica.

The government has organized professional training courses for about a dozen journalists while other journalists have taken courses abroad or participated in seminars on journalism sponsored by international institutes.

5.1 Present practices

Journalism of opinion, which is so close to the essay and traditional literature in Latin America, is quite effective although the work of research and verification which would give it depth is frequently lacking. Editorials and columns expressing personal views are common and have proven impact on the audience. What is most lacking is interpretative or educational journalism and this might in turn be attributed to the lack of inclination or of time for study and research concerning subjects of current interest.

Informational journalism is a mixture of modern techniques and vestiges of improvisation and shows the greatest variations in quality. There is a generation of journalists, which has a praiseworthy tradition of service to national causes and a marked influence on the development of Costa Rican society; but their style and approach, which are the result of their self-training, lack the polish given by professionalism and competition. Their self-criticism covers several points.

Some assert that journalists have had no education other than the hard daily work of their job, that they have not given sufficient information in national crises and that they share the defects of the political and social régime.

Others state that journalists must go beyond the level of the mere reporters who gather bulletins or hearsay from official sources rather than investigate the causes and effects of the events which he reports. A third complaint is that the journalist employs rudimentary techniques adopted by intuition rather than through study. Finally, some leaders confess to a certain disdain for journalism which, according to them, exaggerates or lacks in credibility or is incapable of analysing the future development of the country in depth and with perspective.

On the other hand, the journalists defend the historic role they have fulfilled in promoting the liberties and values of Costa Rican society, and many intellectuals support them. The fraternity has been subject to political and economic pressures which it has resisted in a professional manner and it has to defend itself against abusive applications of the press law when it has criticized the conduct of public figures.

Amongst the most notable cases are those of the candidate Daniel Oduber against *La Nación*, President José Figueres against Rolando Angulo and, more recently, that of the deputy Sigurd Koberg against Rodrigo Madrigal.

Finally, it was the journalists themselves who support the founding of the Colegio de Periodistas (Society of Journalists) and the Escuela de Ciencias de la Comunicación Colectiva (School of Mass Communication Sciences).

5.2 **Society of Journalists**

According to the organic law which established it in September 1969, the Colegio de Periodistas de Costa Rica (Society of Journalists) is a corporation made up of professionals who are authorized to practise journalism in the country, as their principal paid occupation, for a periodical publication, an electronic news medium or a news agency.

Writers and also photographers who practised the profession for five years prior to the promulgation of the law were incorporated in the Society. From the date of its foundation, only graduates of the school or those whose studies abroad are approved by the school are admitted to membership. The law does not require that commentators or writers for specialized magazines or those engaged in similar activities on radio or television should be members of the Society but it does require that directors of mass media and also public relations officers of official bodies should be members.

The aims of the Society include the promotion of the study of the sciences of the communication, the stimulation of popular culture, the furthering of the Society's unity and of the progress of the profession, the protection of its interests and the provision of medical and social assistance and retirement benefits for its members and their families.

The Society must also 'contribute to the development of the democratic republican régime, defend national sovereignty and the institutions of the nation and make known its views on public problems'.

The code of ethics adopted by the Society in June 1973 (for the implementations of which there is a Court of Honour), requires that the journalist should be in the service of 'freedom for the truth, responsibility in expression ... and greater justice in the distribution of access to and enjoyment of science and culture (for all) in the interests of human dignity and freedom'.

The code affirms that sources of information must remain confidential as a professional secret and that freedom of information must be defended 'as a basic human right'.

In his 1973 report, the president of the Society, Rolando Angulo, described the work to be undertaken in the first years as follows:

To overcome a certain degree of division and indifference amongst journalists, and to distinguish between the functions of the Union which has existed ever since the time of the Association of Journalists which preceded the Society and the latter body.

To resist political pressures by the parties, the Congress and government officials, exerted with reference to the law on the right of reply, the legislation concerning taxes on advertising and other discussions on legislation.

To resist initiatives by groups which are considered to be without direct links with the profession but which are interested in advantages connected with the Society: advertising agents, writers and authors, and sports announcers not connected with radio news programmes.

To oppose the practice of some enterprises which employ journalists who are not members of the Society.

To support Press Week in order to raise the status of the journalist and to arrange for competitions and prizes to stimulate his advancement.

The most positive achievement was the obtaining of approval for the law for the financing of the Society by means of a 1 per cent tax on the media's revenues from commercial advertising which was promulgated in April 1974 in spite of the opposition of the agencies and a certain political storm which it set off. The Society has also undertaken to grant an annual subsidy from this new income to the School of Journalism to enable the latter to finance specific projects.

Up to that time, the modest subscriptions of the members had hardly met operating expenses; now the Society is contemplating financing its own building, scholarships and exchanges, research work and the publication of journalistic works.

5.3 The School of Mass Communication Sciences

On the initiative of the Association of Journalists of Costa Rica, which preceded the Society, the School of Journalism was founded in 1968, and although it had neither sufficient resources nor specialized teachers it began to give systematic training in various aspects of communication. The first courses were excessively literary and devoted too much attention to cultural generalities without concentrating on the techniques of journalism as such.

The dissatisfaction of some members of the Society and of the University of Costa Rica where it functioned led to the evaluation seminar at the end of 1973, the principal recommendations of which for a reform of programmes and functions were:

1. To initiate as soon as possible research work in fields vital to journalistic activity in the Costa Rican region. The knowledge gained would make possible the reorientation of programmes, methods and techniques for the education of communicators as agents of change and development rather than as simple reporters.
2. To set up the laboratories essential for education and experimentation in the techniques of written and electronic communication and possibly of cinematography and to build up a specialized library.
3. To initiate the professionalization of the empirical journalists of the Society by means of special courses and collaboration with the Society in joint projects for scholarships and research and campaigns for the improvement of the profession.
4. To convene a national conference for the definition of development aims in Costa Rica in terms of which the university and the school will be able to define their own roles in this national enterprise.

A controversy which was set off towards the middle of 1974 by accusations in the press to the effect that the school allowed some of its teachers 'to give instruction in their classes on Marxist principles' served to clarify ideas. The highest organ of the school, the University Council, and a meeting of students and teachers of the school refuted the charges, confirmed academic freedom and defended the integrity of the foreign teachers who were attacked.

The controversy, which involved the weekly newspaper *Universidad* and the daily *La Nación* as well as the school, gave rise to other observations such as the following:

Most of the teachers worked according to their time-table and did not pay sufficient attention to the needs of the students and this was true also of the director. Some teachers did not prepare their courses.

It was necessary to bring the school out of the stage of 'experimental stammering' and diversity of programmes—full of general culture only marginally related to journalism—and raise it to the position of a centre for research and for the theoretical and practical teaching of journalism and training in the use of the language of communication and its various media.

It was necessary to improve the selection and quality of the students, to test their sense of vocation and academic orientation and to reorganize their empirical knowledge.

Professor Javier Solís, the director since the middle of 1973, recognized the problems created by a low budget, a body of teachers with more goodwill than time available and training in journalism, the lack of laboratories and ill-directed programmes. For the end of that same year, contracts had been signed with six outside teachers, two of them to teach full time.

A commission drew up new programmes with a new methodology and a new journalistic orientation. The first projects such as those for an editorial room, a specialized library and an audio-visual laboratory, were being worked out for the end of 1974 and were to be financed by subsidies from the Society.

The new programmes entered into force in 1974, and their declared objective is to 'qualify communicators for the transmission of culture by means of professional education in scientific, technical and humanistic fields'. In fact the plan included the following: (a) the sciences of mass communication, together with research projects; (b) techniques and criteria acquired in theoretical and practical courses in written, electronic and later, cinematographic journalism with specialization in the third year; (c) social and humanistic training so that the communicator will understand the environment in which his work is done.

The courses include philosophy (logic), Spanish, the history of culture, elements of biology or mathematics, principles of psychology and economics, Costa Rican institutions, and introduction to the sciences of mass communication, all in the pre-professional (or general studies) year.

For the first professional year: theory of communication, methods of research, grammar, theory and practice of journalism, dealing with news, press legislation.

In the second year: sociology of communication, linguistics and semiology, grammar, photographic techniques, graphic journalism, interpretative journalism, radio and television techniques, national problems.

Third year: laboratory, Costa Rican literature, current economic problems, composition and layout, printing processes and techniques; laboratory for written journalism; correct pronunciation (radio and television), radio and television production and editing; radio and television laboratory; advertising organization and practice, principles of public relations.

Fourth year: research laboratory, professional ethics, art criticism, administration of an enterprise, laboratory for radio and television journalism, programming, advertising, public relations, marketing.

At the end of the fourth year, the student may write a thesis for the degree of licentiate if he has gained 175 credits including optional courses. At the end of the third year, he can gain the *bachillerato* with 140 credits in science, techniques and social training. Specialization in press, radio and television begins at this point. The optional courses cover contemporary political thought, theory of power, pressure groups in society, history of Costa Rica, macro-economics, history of journalism, scientific journalism, rural information, collective psychology and social typology; cybernetics or philosophy of the sciences, communication technology, architecture and design. The programme also includes, as obligatory, sports, history of art, one of two foreign languages and supplementary seminars.

The programme is more exacting in its requirements for entry and in the course preparatory to the years of professional study.

The controversy and the seminar on evaluation served to clarify ideas on the school, amongst them those of its director, Professor Solís, who observed:

In order to turn the school for reporters into a school for communicators our present project is to the effect that, after two years of general subjects, there shall be specialization in the various communication techniques. But everything should be related to a message, like communicating vessels for the culture of the people, not in any erudite sense but in the sense of the values upon which our society is based.

He has previously affirmed the need for research to determine these values, the currents they inspire, the conflicts that affect them and the goals to be attained at the national level. He added: 'We lack studies on the present state of the press, on the cultural penetration of radio and on content analysis. The sole effort in this direction was the book *La Dominación Cultural en el Subdesarrollo* (Cultural Domination in Underdevelopment). The author of the book is Professor Daniel Camacho, Dean of the Faculty of Social Sciences.

Other responsible figures in communication are in agreement that, although progress has slowly been made since the society and the school have begun to function, fundamental defects such as empiricism and lack of comprehension continue to exist and these defects are most harmful when the intention is to give information on events which are vital for society and to shed light on negative or positive factors in the dynamic of its development.

5.4 Other professional tasks

Communication by means of radio and television and the few films which are produced depends on experience gained from written journalism together with a few 'imported' techniques learned by analogy. In addition to this, there is the feeling that audio-visual journalism has more effect on audiences.

Radio news broadcasts have, however, moved from the stage of printed models to the aggressive dynamism characteristic of the radio medium, while several of the journalists who are working in television today come from the radio news programmes. In the little film activity which is carried on, the cameramen learned their profession by imitation, while the soundmen learned theirs in radio and the director in the theatre.

The general obstacle to professional improvement is the high cost of the transfer of the relevant technology, whether this means teachers who have to be trained in the more advanced markets of Europe and North America or equipment implant.

In the advertising field, executives learned their techniques in business administration and on visits abroad. The craftsmen (draughtsmen, designers and planners) and the artisans have not gone beyond the *bachillerato* in secondary school, except for a few who have taken courses in the fine arts. These benefit from the widespread display of advertising material laid before the public by foreign enterprises.

Another field in which further studies are needed is that of public relations which are being increasingly used in both the private and the public sector. One of the healthy effects of the presence of a larger number of journalists in these posts is the change from the defensive concept of always selling a good image to the realistic concept which presents the good side but recognizes defects.

In the graphic arts, which supplement simple communications with an entire range of posters, pamphlets, programmes, leaflets and other work, professional training takes place through the apprentice system under old workshop foremen whose predecessors were trained abroad. The introduction of offset printing and electronic systems has made it necessary to send technicians abroad for further training.

6 Participation of the public

In spite of the fact that the relationship between the media and their various audiences is the essential aspect of the process of mass communication, it is very difficult to measure it and this is also true of the mutual influence which they can exert.

An audience—a mass or definite group—is guided by values, images, stereotypes and ideologies which react to specific facts, persons, situations or statements, and the communicators themselves use various approaches. It is thus almost impossible to predict or define the relationship.

The changing attitudes of the public are precisely what makes up public opinion, which is formed by discussion and intellectual exchange of positions. It can relate to biological requirements, such as the purity of the water of a certain piping system or complex ideologies such as the question which party or system of ideas is best from the point of view of the government of the country.

Furthermore, the political sciences, social psychology and anthropology, which are valuable aids to the sciences of mass communication, confirm that the media cannot always arrive at a consensus as to the truth. In the months preceding the Revolution of 1948, opposing groups knew, and recognized in private, that the opposition was to some extent right and possessed some merits in regard to the vital questions which led to the conflict at that time but they nevertheless denied it in public and, for reasons of political tactics, attacked the position taken up by the other side.[1]

Moreover, although the idea of the 'common good' predominates as the principal goal of the communicator, it is difficult to define its characteristic features; some authors consider it an intangible value of society which varies according to the interests of the group or sector. For example, the common good is one thing for trade union leaders and another for the financiers who control production.

Finally, events with a national impact such as a rise in the price of milk, the recovery of property held without clear title, a scandal concerning a public figure, affect readers, listeners and viewers differently and hold their interest to a degree depending upon the depth of their emotions and

---

1. John Patrick Bell's *Crisis in Costa Rica—The Revolution of 1948* (Institute of Latin American Studies, The University of Texas at Austin, 1972) goes further into this subject.

their capacity for paying attention so long as no other more important event occurs. Public opinion is influenced also by differences in social position, culture, age, sex, profession and loyalties. Broadly speaking, there are publics which prefer immediate pleasure (the superficial) to a more distant satisfaction of a higher nature.

In regard to opinion as the motive force that generates development, account must be taken of the fidelity, frequency and skill in synthesizing with which the communicators convey the ideas of leaders and experts. It is at the level of those ideas and concepts that the people can be influenced so as to be guided towards the goals of social and cultural improvement. After an honest discussion of these questions by leaders and experts they can arrive at a consensus, but this consensus is dissipated or lost if their message reaches the public in an ambiguous, incomplete or distorted form.

6.1 Communicators

Relations between communicators and the public assume different forms, according to this survey:

There is a tacit agreement between the communicators and the public for the dissemination of information which contributes to the discussion of social problems and aims and to the development of the country.

There is a passive and purely receptive relationship between the public and the media whose information it accepts and to whose advertising it pays attention.

When the content and presentation are critical (denunciations, protest) there is more public participation and some groups mobilize themselves politically.

The public participates in the formation of opinion on subjects of current interest by means of letters or telephone calls to the media and by co-operation in interviews and surveys. The expression of views in controversies is another form of participation.

One communicator (Rolando Angulo) mentioned credibility as the basis of the relationship when he stated:

We have been mindful to preserve our credibility and the people respect us. What we transmit must be confirmed and reliable news. We measure the impact by the number of letters and calls from people from different sectors.

Several of the communicators, which were questioned in the survey, spoke of the need to avoid sensationalism and exaggeration. Others mentioned 'empathy' when speaking of the sector of the public which 'identifies' itself with a medium because it reproduces situations within the grasp of the average reader or radio listener. Some columns and sections such as the 'Do Re Mi' column of *La República* and the sports reports are widely accepted.

The communicators are of the opinion that the influence of the medium on the public is greater than that of the public on the medium. This is especially true of television programmes which, it is generally recognized, have produced changes in the attitudes, habits and language of viewers.

Finally, it is worth mentioning that value of controversy as a form of public participation in the media which is so great that foreign writers have gone so far as to assert that the Costa Rican press is largely 'produced' by the public.

6.2 Opinion of secondary school pupils

A survey (carried out in 1971 by professors of the University of Costa Rica) among 256 fourth-year secondary school pupils showed their level of exposure to the media and their opinion of the content. The survey covered 113 girls and 143 boys. The principal findings were as follows:

All have a radio receiver at home which 59 per cent of the boys and 65 per cent of the girls listened to regularly (radio news programmes) on school days. As to the printed media, 96 per cent of the boys and 95 per cent of the girls read the newspaper. Magazines or weeklies are read by 56 per cent of the boys and 65 per cent of the girls and 70 per cent of the boys and 65 per cent of the girls read books in addition to those mentioned by the school.

An average of 91 per cent have a television set at home, and watch television for almost two hours per day during the week. Of those included in the survey, 81 per cent go to the cinema on an average of five times every two months. About 36 per cent have a telephone.

For those covered by the survey, Radio Reloj supplies the best information (it is preferred by 70 per cent), while Radio Monumental follows (with 17 per cent). As to the extent to which radio broadcasting is of service to young people, approximately 38 per cent of the boys are of the opinion that it is positively so and 41 per cent of the girls agree. On the other hand, 61 per cent of the boys believe that its value as a service is negative and 58 per cent of the girls are of the same opinion. The majority therefore do not believe that radio serves their interests.

Of those who believe that radio performs a positive service, 22 per cent of the boys and 20 per cent of the girls recognize its cultural and educational aspects while 18 per cent and 25 per cent respectively recognize its value as a source of information. Of the boys 13 per cent find radio entertaining while of the girls 5 per cent agree.

In addition, 13 per cent of the boys are of the opinion that radio deals with social problems of interest to young people; but only 4 per cent find that it deals with specific problems such as sex, drugs or delinquency. Of the girls, 5 per cent appreciated the treatment given to social problems and 7 per cent said that the radio treats specific problems.

Of the sector of those included in the survey who denied that radio is of service to young people, 17 per cent were of the opinion that it should give a cultural and educational message; 50 per cent considered that it should pay attention to the problems of youth and 3.5 per cent wished for attention to be paid to very specific problems (for both groups, boys and girls).

As to the press, those covered by the survey preferred *La Nación* (better information, 77 per cent). *La República* comes next (preferred by 10 per cent), but 53 per cent of the young people said that the daily press does not deal with their interests, problems and needs. Of the girls, 41 per cent share the negative opinion but 50 per cent consider that it does deal with their interests. In addition, 8 per cent of the boys consider that the press offers a good amount of cultural and educational content and some 7 per cent of the girls agree. Of the boys, 25 per cent believe that it provides good information (complete) while 39 per cent of the girls agree. Of the boys 36 per cent consider that the press deals with the problems of youth as do 28 per cent of the girls.

For problems such as sex, drugs and delinquency, the percentages are 2 per cent and 7 per cent respectively.

Of those having a negative opinion of the press, some 8 per cent of the boys and 2 per cent of the girls consider that it should include a greater educational and cultural content while 52 per cent of the boys and 65 per cent of the girls wish for more attention to the problems of young people and 5 per cent and 8 per cent respectively would like education concerning the problems of sex, drugs and delinquency.

In another category, 6 per cent stated in the questionnaire that they wanted the press to give more attention to national problems of general interest.

In addition to offering a typology of young people on the threshold of their entry into adult society, the survey supplies data on differences in opinion according to sex which are however slight, and confirms the 'communicative' character of students. It also reveals the strength of reading habits and that more is demanded from the press than from the radio. There were no questions concerning television programmes.

6.3 University students and the media

Another survey at the University of Costa Rica in 1973 concerning the weekly *Universidad* and other media collected data on the socio-economic and cultural typology of students, the use of their time and the degree of 'empathy' and interest in various events according to their origin and category. This study considered empathy (the intraspective capacity to understand the situation of others) to be important since it is an essential element of communication and social solidarity. It also measured to what degree those included in the survey find the various media to be credible.

A team of fourteen third-year students of the 'Media Research' course[1] consulted 200 of the 20,000 university students in a random sample. A questionnaire consisting of twelve questions on media content, use of time, information preferences, personal data and opinion on national and international subjects served as a basis for the survey. Those carrying out the survey were instructed as to the principle of the mutual independence between all the mass media factors and the play of reciprocal influences (events, communicator, vehicle, receiver) so that they would treat the audience (university students) as an active rather than an indifferent entity with a capacity for opinions and critical reactions.

The researchers could thus test the view that the reader is a thinking being, with an active psychological and mental structure, influenced by his own experience concerned with problems, stimulated by achievements and challenges and motivated by impelling values.

The morphology of *Universidad* was described as that of a tabloid of sixteen to twenty pages with an average edition of 5,000 copies, with 15 per cent of its space given over to advertisements (the university itself, the government, book-shops, publishers) and with a content more educational than informational, as is appropriate for a weekly in the service of a community of scholars. At the time of the survey, *Universidad* contained many feature articles, items of news, interviews and comments on national problems and those of Latin America and its approach was of a critical and reformist nature. The editorial staff consists of students of the School of Mass Communication Sciences. The director and several collaborators are teachers at the same university. It publishes texts of lectures given on Radio Universitaria as part of the courses, so that many students are obliged to read it. Politics and social problems predominate in the content of the weekly along with some art and science.

6.3.1 *Typology*

Of the group of university students consulted, 45 per cent were from 21 to 25 years of age, 32 per cent less than 20 years of age and 0.6 per cent from 26 to 30. Of these 60 per cent were men. Of the total number, 12 per cent had spent five years at the university, 14 per cent four years, 22 per cent three years and 13 per cent two years. First-year students made up 15 per cent. As to the subject-matter, 12 per cent took courses in general studies, 7 per cent in agronomy, 6 per cent in philosophy, 5.4 per cent in law, 5.4 per cent in psychology, 5.2 per cent in journalism, 5.2 per cent in medicine, 5 per cent in economics, 4.2 per cent in engineering and 2.4 per cent in sociology. The rest took languages, history and other humanist

---

1. Escuela de Ciencias de la Comunicación, Curso sobre Investigación de Medios (School of Mass Communication Sciences: Course on Research into the Media), 1973. Professor Jaime Fonseca, *Universidad* survey—October, November.

subjects. In the group concerned by the survey the humanities predominated over the sciences.

Of the total number of students, 33 per cent came from middle-class secondary schools, 25 per cent from upper-class schools and 32 per cent from schools in low-income areas.

Of the students, 58 per cent give all their time to their studies while 36 per cent study and work to feed themselves. One-third live in the centre of San José while the majority live in the middle-class suburbs and less than one-third in the provinces. Sixty-two per cent have a telephone, 70 per cent a refrigerator, 94 per cent a radio and 88 per cent have a television set at home and 41 per cent have a motor-car in the family. Of those included in the survey, 40 per cent have from four to seven brothers or sisters, another 40 per cent have less than four and 14 per cent more than seven.

The time-tables of the group questioned are as follows: two to ten hours weekly are given over to study by 25 per cent of the university students; to reading by 58 per cent; to work by 9 per cent; to resting by 28 per cent; to sport by 49 per cent and entertainment (cinema, walks, music or dancing) by 52 per cent. From ten to twenty hours weekly are given over to study by 27 per cent; to reading by 10 per cent; to work by 12 per cent; to resting by 9 per cent; to sport by 2.5 per cent; and to entertainment by rather more than 11 per cent. From twenty to forty hours weekly are given over to study by 19 per cent; to reading by 1 per cent; to work by 9 per cent; to resting by 15 per cent; to sport by 15 per cent; and to entertainment by rather more than 4 per cent. More than forty hours a week are employed in the following ways: study, 13 per cent; reading, 0 per cent; work, 9 per cent; and resting 28 per cent.

6.3.2 *Information*

The university audience displayed the following trends:

The source of information was the daily press for 81 per cent, radio for 34 per cent and television programmes for 24 per cent, although none of these means were used exclusively since information was received from several media by turns.

Information was received from fellow students and friends by 60 per cent and from the family by 30 per cent. Information was derived from magazines by 29 per cent while 15 per cent sought information in specialized publications (cinema, sports, hobbies, etc.), and 58 per cent said that they went to the cinema regularly.

Preferences concerning the sources of news were as follows: the university, 32 per cent; the city, 14 per cent; the nation, 60 per cent; the world, 41 per cent. It will be recalled that the newspapers publish information which in the average is 63 per cent national news and 37 per cent world news.

As for subjects or activities, the students' preferences were: politics and administration, 58 per cent; economics, 37 per cent; social questions, 51 per cent; cultural matters, 40 per cent; sports, 28 per cent and entertainment, 13 per cent. The newspapers publish a great deal of material on politics, a fair amount on economic subjects and little on social questions.

The questionnaire ascertained the medium through which the persons included in the first received their information concerning news items previously selected on the ground of their importance and origin. The results were as follows:

Source and news items	Means of communication and percentage of students				
	Universidad	Newspapers	Radio	Television	'I was told'
University					
Election of the rector	40	50	10	3	16
Student Congress	36	14	5.4	0.6	24
Thefts in the university	21	25	4.2	0	26
Nation					
Transfer of petroleum refinery from multi-national ownership to government	12	80	18	6	0
Rape of minors	2	64	20	3	2
Meat shortage	10	70	24	5	0
World					
Military coup in Chile	17	52	52	13	0
Nixon-Watergate crisis	9	77	16	4	0
War in the Middle East	10	65	34	7	0

The newspapers are the principal source of information for the majority of the university students questioned, except for news with an internal impact such as the election of the rector or the student congress while radio news broadcasts come next and television programmes last.

In addition, the question of the credibility placed in the various media was asked in the following manner: 'What degree of confidence do you have in the information given by . . . ?' The results (as percentages) are shown in the following table:

	Universidad[1]	Nación	República	Diario de C.R.	Prensa Libre	Radio news	Television news	Magazines
'A great deal'	40	21	17	9	10	17	25	27
'Little'	35	59	41	40	43	40	32	30
'None'	1	4	1	2	2	2	1	1
'Do not know'	24	16	41	49	45	41	32	30
No reply							10	12

1. Those questioned attribute a high degree of credibility to the weekly *Universidad* since it is connected with their community. . . . They can check what is published by direct reference to the sources; the editorial staff are students and the director is a professor which 'identifies' them better with campus readers. At the same time, the latter can influence some of its policies and can take it for granted that it will report their strikes, protests and other 'domestic' events. Since it does not depend entirely upon advertisements, the student readers know that the weekly can be independent as to its opinion and information content.

6.4 Lack of communication by marginal sectors

Approximately one-third of the population of Costa Rica suffer from the effects of the 'lack of mass communication' and are marginal sectors from the point of view of society as regards transmitting or receiving communication. This one-third does not fully share in the supply of information handled by the media. It accepts and uses some aspects of it but does not depend on this supply or contribute to it except by accident (crimes, disputes about land). This is a marginal sector supplying its own values and communication signal in order to survive. To a slight extent some news with 'meaning' or significance for the poor filters through by osmosis from the neighbouring 'upper' strata such as, for example, a food crisis or national elections. These 'communicationless' groups communicate above all 'orally' (person to person, family to family, group to group or gang) with a terminology belonging to the culture of the poor.

Some authorities calculate that the marginal groups make up 52 per cent of the total population of the country, while others consider that they constitute approximately two-thirds. In fact, 75 per cent of the wage-earning population have a monthly income of about $70 per family (although the average income per person is approximately $650 annually). There are islands of poverty in the urban concentrations and sometimes whole city centres which grow as the result of immigration from the countryside. It is in the rural areas, however, that the labourers and the so-called 'squatters' live in even worse conditions. The squatter is the landless peasant who occupies a plot of land without a legal right to do so, that is to say, on precarious tenure. At the beginning of the decade of the 1970s, 57 per cent of the land in the country was occupied without legal right to its possession.

As far as school attendance and illiteracy are concerned, Costa Rica devotes 30 per cent of its governmental budget to education; and the rate of urban literacy has reached 97 per cent and that of rural literacy 84 per cent.

Even under these conditions, the average for school attendance is four years, 54 per cent of the children of school age do not get further than the primary grade and 20 per cent do not attend school at all. The government is endeavouring to extend school attendance, increase vocational training (technical) and reduce the number of school drop-outs.

The lack of access to the printed media in the marginal sector is partially compensated by the transistor radio although the supply of information comes second amongst listeners' preferences, the first place being taken by music and entertainment. There is also cultural exchange because of the relative smallness of the territory and the growing network of roads and air links.

This exchange is easier on the Central Plateau which, although it occupies barely one-fifth of the territory, has been the demographic magnet where 58 per cent of the total population is now concentrated. The metropolitan area of San José contains one quarter of the 2 million inhabitants. The remaining 42 per cent live in localities with 2,000 or more inhabitants or in villages and hamlets.

Obviously the daily and weekly newspapers circulate in greater numbers in this central zone. The ratio of one copy to eight inhabitants which is reached in the Central Plateau falls off in the zones outside this area to one copy per 100 inhabitants.

6.4.1 *Lack of cultural communication*

Although some information bridgeheads penetrate the isolation of the marginal sectors, the truth is that these sectors do not fully receive the message of the newspapers and other media as these are principally directed towards the city and its values. The press and radio and television news programmes respond better to the play of interests, reasoning and emotions of the urban groups whose common denominator is the comfort of the consumer society. Their message selects facts according to their affinity and excludes situations, needs and aspirations of the marginal sector except when the latter takes part in social conflict.

Thus, the 'non-communication' groups create and live in 'their world', going their way in the penumbra of the national life where the popular leaders and agents of development operate when there are programmes which lead them to attempt to come to an understanding with those in the marginal sectors.

Recently there has been an attempt to establish communication between those in charge of development projects for the relief of poverty and the victims of poverty, with a view to directing mental attitudes and motivations towards 'overcoming' poverty. The Instituto Mixto de Ayuda Social (IMAS) (Mixed Institute for Social Aid), in collaboration with the Faculty of Education of the University of Costa Rica, making use of an educational development programme of the Organization of American States, has begun to train specialists in raising the standard of the marginal classes. The relevant project states:

> At the present time, a group of professionals, technicians and others who are working for change and who are promoting the development and advancement of the poorer classes have seen their efforts hampered or reduced to little effect by the absence of procedures, techniques and means by which their professional level could be equated with the limitations imposed upon the supposed beneficiaries of those programmes. These limitations apply to concepts, perception, psychomotor reactions, ideological schematization and projection in praxis. This situation affects especially those in the marginal groups, in cities as well as in country districts.

IMAS defines its housing programme as being devised to provide 'space in which to prepare food, rest, work and carry on social life in a humanizing environment'. Adequate social communication between those working for the changes and the poor helps towards the attainment of the same goal, namely, that of meeting the biological and spiritual needs of the human being.

A first course of training for development (lasting more than three months and ending in April 1975), in which eighteen communal leaders participated, led to innovations in the teaching of those working for the social improvement of the marginal groups, and to the introduction of studies on their 'habitat' and their attitudes and motivations and started to compile a terminology of poverty. The object of these efforts was to discover and cultivate the 'operational' factors in the basic community: rudimentary forms of co-operation, self-improvement, association, service, and leadership for a group dynamic directed towards development.

6.4.2 *Samples of marginal groups*

A demographic study (a field in which there have been important compaigns in recent years) revealed that the inhabitants of a village (Cajón in the district of Pérez Zeledón) have more confidence in the radio than in the doctor or nurse so far as birth control methods are concerned. The credibility percentages for the villagers covered by the survey were: in the radio, 65 per cent; in the doctor, 7 per cent; in the nurse, 3 per cent; in programmes of the medical care unit (clinic), 5 per cent; in other media, 3 per cent; no reply, 17 per cent. Why there seems to be more empathy or identification between radio-communicator and radio-listener than between villager and specialist is a question that should be studied.

Another study carried out by students of journalism in April 1973 (Luis A. Montoya and associates) was a survey of two groups of urban population, Aguantafilo with 120 dwellings and Chapulines with fifty (both in San José) where IMAS was carrying out improvements in housing and communal organization. The object was to determine the typology of the inhabitants and the possible influence on them of the media.

In Aguantafilo, 89 per cent of the population came from rural regions; 51 per cent said they had emigrated in order to improve their income, 12 per cent their health, and 12 per cent in order to rejoin their families. Of the families, 63 per cent have five children and there was an average of seven persons per household. In 64 per cent of the families the head of the household was a man or husband and in 36 per cent a woman alone. Of the heads of households, 61 per cent worked while none of the women had any fixed employment. In Aguantafilo 75 per cent of those capable of working were unemployed.

A radio receiver was owned and listened to regularly by 57 per cent and 16 per cent had a television set, while the rest received their information orally. Of the population of school age, 41 per cent attended primary school, 7 per cent secondary school and 2 per cent the university.

The most conservative daily newspaper was read by 32 per cent, the evening tabloid papers by 7 per cent; and more than 50 per cent read the communist paper, which was distributed free, and 3 per cent the socialist weekly. Of the total, 56 per cent stated that they believed in the media they used.

In Chapulines, 34 per cent of the population were born in the district and 66 per cent came from other places, 38 per cent for economic reasons, 4 per cent for health reasons and 12 per cent for family reasons. In each dwelling here also there was an average of seven persons, although the number of children varies between four and five. The husband is present in 76 per cent of the households while in 18 per cent there are women and children without a male breadwinner. The unemployment index is 42 per cent (the percentage for the nation as a whole varied between 10 per cent and 12 per cent during those months).

Radio was listened to by 70 per cent and television watched by 28 per cent. Of the population of school age, 31 per cent attended primary school, 14 per cent secondary school and 1 per cent the university.

Of the literate population, 66 per cent read the newspaper regularly and of this group 46 per cent preferred the most conservative paper, 6 per cent read newspapers with more balanced information, 28 per cent the communist organ which they buy and 8 per cent the socialist paper. The media are considered credible by 62 per cent.

Unfortunately, this research did not include other studies or surveys concerning rural population groups in the process of urbanization.

All these surveys indicate the complexity and diversity of the audience-publics and therefore the variations in their relations with the media and the degree of mutual influence. The figures for credibility, for example, range from 56 per cent for some marginal groups to 80 per cent for students, while listening to the radio is more frequent amongst the marginal groups and less amongst students. While up to 90 per cent of the more literate population depend upon newspapers for their information, only 25 per cent of the marginal groups do so and they, in any case, seem to prefer a conservative content rather than a message containing social demands.

It is worth while mentioning briefly the interest taken in characteristic customs and the strong tradition of folklore in Costa Rican journalism which inherited from them turns of speech, images and situations of a typically peasant nature. Descriptions of customs and political criticism were important features of the first newspapers in the country and still persist in the press and in radio programmes.

6.5 Social solidarity and opinion

The controversy between two schools of thought concerning public opinion in Costa Rica is an important element in an evaluation of public participation in the media.

One school of historians, sociologists and writers supports the idea of a united society which, through free and public discussion by the mass media, succeeds in overcoming the tensions inherent in any human group.

In opposition to this school, there is the criticism of the left which points to the existence in Costa Rican society of a series of contradictions and short-comings or defects originating precisely in those sectors which are represented in the mass media. Together they engender social conflict which sometimes remains latent and sometimes breaks out. The sectors in question are power groups and pressure groups.

The proponents of the united society assert that Costa Rica constitutes 'a real nation' and is conscious of this historical phenomenon. *La Nación* explains this as follows (10 June 1974):

To be a nation means that each inhabitant who dwells in a given independent territory as a national feels himself to be part of a common destiny and identifies his own existence with that of his country. ... There is consciousness of nationality in all classes and sectors of the country overriding social levels, political parties, geographical zones and human conditions. That the wounds from internal struggles heal so quickly and that the bitter hatreds and irreconcilable passions of a given moment subside within a short time and are even forgotten is a phenomenon which surprises many but which has its ultimate explanation in the extraordinary fact that our people is a nation.

The concept of nationality attributes political stability and the capacity for reconciliation, even after conflicts such as the civil war of 1948, to this civic cohesiveness. Another representative of this school, León Pacheco (in the magazine *Combate*, April 1961), enumerates the components of this democracy as follows:

The almost complete absence of indigenous population during the three colonial centuries, which contributed to the creation of a rural society without castes.
The multiplication and consolidation of small agricultural property, the '*finca*', through the spontaneous colonizing expansion of the citizens without State direction or dictation.
The absence of religious struggles as a result of the delimitation of the civil and religious fields.
The predominance of civilian governments because the military caste did not gain power and the consequent concentration of resources on peaceful objects with priority being given to public education.

The critical school of the left became more prominent in the 1930s and grew important towards the middle of the century when, for economic reasons, a managerial middle class appeared as a result of foreign investments in the country, the importance of which increased when efforts were directed towards ensuring central American economic integration. The criticism coincided with the development of the power of advertising and the imbalance between real production and consumption. It took the following form:

The high level of education and economic and social mobility, backed by political stability, attract new investments mainly in industry, to a lesser extent in agriculture and to some degree in stock-raising. North American capital is the source of 85 per cent of the investments in new industries while the amount of coffee plantation capital in national production and revenue is falling. Foreign investments, together with the fact that many young Costa Ricans are educated abroad, produce a new social group with different values: the managerial middle class which at first has economic influence but has no capital of its own.

In the first place, this middle class is not completely identified with the traditional Costa Rican middle class since it is dependent upon foreign capital but it still has an umbilical relation with Costa Rican culture. For this reason, it suffers from a conflict.

In the second place, the use to which the profits are put also creates a situation of conflict. Because of its legislation and its constitution, the country is deeply committed to reinvesting in the social welfare of the working people through social services, a wages system and social security schemes which must necessarily be financed from profits from industry, agriculture, commerce and other activities. The State therefore requires dividends from investments by both citizens and foreigners to be kept in the country, but the North American and other investors must export a large part if not the whole of their profits or otherwise they lose their incentive and succumb to the competition of other capital markets. José Luis Vega Carballo and Rodolfo Cerdas (in the magazine *Alero*, No. 9, 1972) give the following version of the alternative, a change in the power structure:

> As a result of the rapid growth of industry under the aegis of international capital a new social group was formed within the dominant classes: a managerial middle class linked to that capital which it represents aggressively in commercial transactions and ultimately in political processes.
>
> This managerial middle class attempts to challenge the old class of coffee planters for political and ideological hegemony by manoeuvring on the international plane whence it draws its real power and financial support. . . . It exercises considerable pressure directed towards modifying the political and ideological superstructure appropriate to the agricultural and stock-raising mode of production. Furthermore, it must rapidly conquer better positions in the scale of political power and social prestige in order to create a State in its image and likeness which will be docile to its decisions.

The critical school mentions the following as being in the line of these possible decisions: legislation favourable to the entry of capital, simple bureaucratic procedures, increased freedom of enterprise within the framework of liberal capitalism, a limit to social legislation in order to avoid additional burdens on production and profits, the weakening of the parliamentary process and of the traditional parties and an executive power of the same type as the managerial middle class.

The consumer public which pays the costs of the investments and profits, the dividends from which are sent abroad, is politically the majority: urban and rural workers, small businessmen, professionals, technicians, craftsmen, teachers, clerks and other similar groups. It continues to be loyal to the traditional parties and their leading personalities, with similar pragmatic and ideological positions. The parties of the left have not built up a platform which attracts enough votes to compete with the managerial or coffee-planting middle class. There is a third force which, apart from the political groups, although sometimes making use of them, has been a factor for development and social unification, namely, the technocrats who, with the aid of international social capital (agencies for aid), have constructed infrastructure works and performed basic services through semi-autonomous State institutions (housing, insurance, electrification, land settlement, water supply, banks) and have provided a certain measure of relief from the country's demographic pressures.

The mass communications and their media play an important role in the competition between all these forces within a legal system of freedom of expression which, however, is not always respected.

Some specific cases can be cited in support of expressions of concern about the press, ranging from accusations to the effect that it abuses its freedom in an irresponsible manner to assertions that it is manipulated by power groups. The journalist Armando Vargas (*Universidad*, March 1972) asserted that 'the political power and the economic power exert pressures which keep the press in chains'. He described the violent intervention of the Criminal Investigation Department which, without any judicial order and just because its Director 'thought it desirable', confiscated a special edition concerning demonstrations by students and workers against a governmental agreement with the North American company Alcoa. Another case was that of the radio round table on union rights which was boycotted by the Chamber of Commerce which withdrew advertising from the radio station. A third case was that of the anti-communist 'Movimiento Costa Rica Libre' (Free Costa Rica Movement) which opposed commercial relations between this country and the Soviet Union and exerted direct pressure on newspapers which had not given prominence to this opposition.

Another issue of the same weekly *Universidad*, after an analysis of the costly production process of the mass media and the necessity for them to be linked to private enterprise, commented: 'Only groups possessing economic power can set up a medium and supply information on subjects which interest and concern them. As long as such conditions subsist, freedom of the press is a myth for the majority.' At the end of the article there was a caricature which showed some well-dressed figures working a rotary press which converted newsprint into paper money.

The North American author, Charles Denton,[1] expresses that mass communication is subject to 'the demands, interests and contributions of the upper levels of the population'. He cites amongst other cases that of the Asociación Nacional de Fomento Económico (ANFE) (National Association for Economic Advancement), the newspaper *La Nación* and the Partido Liberación Nacional (National Liberation Party) and their media, and adds:

1. Charles Denton, *La Política del Desarrollo en Costa Rica* [Development Policy in Costa Rica], San José, 1969.

'The press is not an independent entity presenting political news with an objective content. Newspapers and radio and television stations function as part of the arsenal of one or other political entity.'

For the economist and planner Oscar Arias Sánchez,[1] the existence of independent pressure groups 'is due precisely to the weakness of the political parties' and this opinion coincides with one of the observations of the criticism of the left concerning the concept of homogeneous nationality. Arias cites also the ANFE and 'its campaigns for the dissemination of principles and objectives' designed to give a favourable image of businessmen. This is not the only group acting in this way, since even the Marxists engage in public relations work.

In regard to questions of legislation and executive decision, the pressure groups adopt similar tactics. 'At first, they use information and persuasion and only when these techniques fail do they resort to threats or political blackmail,' observes Arias. Some groups claim to represent public opinion and the common good when they are only furthering their own interests, supported by means for propagating their own view. 'In the tactics of persuasion, exaggeration is the very essence of pressure politics. ... Only with the support of a strong and disciplined party can a legislator attempt to resist these pressures,' he adds.

In another content, the Asociación Costarricense de Agencias de Publicidad (Costa Rican Association of Advertising Agencies) intervened when the Assembly discussed the law for consumer protection and stated that it supported 'the consumer and his rights, particularly his right to receive truthful and exact information' concerning advertised products. At the same time, however, it asserted that it is impossible to verify the prices in all cases and it refused to accept any responsibility as to the quality of the products advertised, which were precisely the two key points for those dissatisfied persons who called for the law.

The Church constitutes another pressure group since politics, economics and the social question involve moral questions (collective and individual salvation). This is the premise upheld by Radio Fides, *Eco Católico* and other media, apart from the traditional medium of the pulpit.

Early in 1975, several priests in rural areas called for a fundamental agrarian reform in view of the conditions in which many peasants live. The Church has also supported campaigns concerning marriage, procreation, education and social justice. One bishop, Monsignor Víctor M. Sanabria, took decisive steps, which he backed up with his pastoral letters, to establish legislation in favour of the workers.[2]

1. Oscar Arias Sánchez, *Grupos de Presión* [Pressure Groups], Editorial Costa Rica, 1971.
2. The activities of Monsignor Sanabria in the post-war years and a little earlier are in the book of Ricardo Blanco Segura, *Monseñor Sanabria,* Editorial Costa Rica, San José.

The relative progress of the oecumenical movement (for closer relations between the various creeds) has made it possible for other groups, like the Protestants, to make constructive contributions to the public discussion concerning national objectives and problems. The Christian-Socialist weekly *Pueblo* devotes itself to this object.

A survey by Oliveth Bogantes Hidalgo[1] collected from the bishops the following list of objectives for their communication media. They should be vehicles for disseminating the social doctrine of the Church in the same way as the encyclicals and the second Vatican council; the expression of prophetic denunciation of injustice and sin; the broadcasting of church services by radio and television and act as an instrument exerting moral influence on individual customs and governmental decision.

Another survey by Jaime Fonseca[2] asserted the need to 'desanctify' the concepts of paternalism and submission and replace them by a dynamic of integral salvation and stated:

The twofold notion magnanimity in the rich and powerful and humility in the poor has for many decades past ceased to be a Christian tenet. That is why it has been easy for positivism to present this duality as the pretext advanced for the continuance of exploitation and misery and for members of the privileged caste to check the integral development of the people. ... A deeper consciousness (communication) of the values of human dignity, autonomy, justice and social solidarity must precede all efforts to create an ethic of development precisely through the communication media which consider themselves Christian.

Finally, some sectors of the public and some individuals participate either on their own initiative or in response to stimulation when the mass media or the government in the discharge of their various functions deal with subjects that directly affect them. These are manifestations of opinion rather than the exertion of pressure. Of their influence on the media, it can be said that they can modify positions and attitudes in the presentation of news, so long as they do not touch the vital nerve of the ideological philosophy of the medium in question or the interests of the group which supports it.

---

1. Oliveth Bogantes Hidalgo, *Iglesia y Comunicación* [Church and Communication], thesis, University of Louvain, Belgium, 1971.
2. Jaime Fonseca, *Estudio d ePosibilidad para una Revista Centroamericana* [Feasibility Study for a Central American magazine], January 1967, Union Latinoamericana de Prensa Católica, Montevideo.

7 Conclusions and trends

This study describes the principles and practices of mass communication at the legal, professional and popular levels, but it is obvious that it does not define Costa Rican 'communication policies', which is a task for academic and professional circles and possibly for the government.

The study shows also the needs of the Costa Ricans for intellectual nourishment in the form of truthful information and pertinent interpretations and mentions the efforts which the communicators make to satisfy that need. There is a good percentage of information by comparison with the amount of advertising and also a good percentage of serious material as compared with frivolous material. There are trends towards an affluent consumer society supported partly by excessive credit.

For the rest, mass communication functions in a legal climate of freedom and responsibility, although subject to restrictions imposed in the interests of the power groups.

Research into these matters reveals some deficiencies in professional training and in legislation, which various groups are trying to remedy, more particularly in the case of the law on the press and some chapters of the regulations for radio and television. In the field of education, both formal and environmental, it is necessary to create civic consciousness as to the value of mass communication for a dynamic process of development and democratic coexistence.

The governmental administration, which is doing good work in planning, does not appear to understand fully the potential of mass communication from the point of view of the execution and discussion of its plans. Perhaps the traditional system of freedom is opposed to greater State interference in the handling of communication which is now in the hands of private enterprises. In the academic field, some faculties of the two universities (in addition to the Universidad de Costa Rica in San Pedro near San José, there is the Universidad Nacional in Heredia) are engaged in studying and stimulating the influence of communication but not even the Escuela de Ciencias de la Comunicación (School of Mass Communication Sciences) has produced the research necessary for demonstrating this influence.

Recently the Ministerio de Cultura, Juventud y Deporte (Ministry of Culture, Youth and Sport) recognized the need to provide regulations for certain programmes on television and other media directed towards young people and children as well as other material for adults of a low cultural level. It collected arguments from various sources in support of the view that most of these programmes are pernicious and perverse and also show excessive foreign influence. A law drawn up by this Ministry proposes the creation of an authority for providing regulations and guidance, the so-called Consejo Costarricense de Radio y Televisión (Costa Rican Radio and Television Council) whose chief duty it would be to raise the educational and cultural level of the programmes and ensure the objectivity of the news broadcasts.

As was to be expected, this regulative activity has encountered a good deal of opposition in most of the communication media.

A small group of communicators and educators agree in affirming the need to develop a sociology of Costa Rican culture in order to apply it in determining and fostering the innate tendency of the nation to better its cultural, social and economic situation (*superación*). Once this has been achieved, the media might be more conscious of national goals tending towards the realization of a civilized and democratic community capable of overcoming the inevitable problems, due to the process of development, demographic pressure and the general economic recession.

Another task which is considered essential would be to determine the country's degree of dependence upon information from the external world, its impact on society and the various ideologies which it represents: traditional capitalism, neo-capitalism, Third World, Soviet bloc, neutral countries. Those who draw attention to this further need consider that the international information message and its impact on society will inevitably be factors in all future planning or formulation of policies.

A third task is to determine to what extent the national audience can absorb the total supply of information: that is to say, whether the various publics are sufficiently prepared to understand and assimilate the entire message or only a selection that is minimal in relation to the resources drawn upon, the volume of information opposed and the effort exerted by the various media; and whether possible 'saturation' does not rather make more difficult for the reader, listener or viewer, the process of 'socially and existentially finding his place' and deciding how to readjust himself either immediately or gradually.

In this connexion, the intensity with which certain social forces act at times of 'national crisis' (such as the revolution of 1948) should be recalled. What degree of professionalism and experience and what ethical standards do all those concerned in the mass media—owner, communicators, instructors—need in order to answer this challenge and consequently to direct news in accordance with objectives possessing the highest priority and to avoid increasing tensions leading to even broader conflict?

In 1975, the School of Mass Communication Sciences initiated the second cycle of reforms planned in 1974 (see Chapter 5). The Society of Journalists became stronger economically as a result of the tax law on advertising (it financed the purchase of a building for itself and began additional programmes). Those who took part in the legislative activity have promised to publish a pamphlet giving the history of the law.

The controversy concerning the nature and the functions of the school broke out again towards the middle of 1975. The view that without properly trained teachers with more time for their academic tasks, the reforms and the very existence of the institution would be of little use gained ground but the work of the school continued.

The newspaper *Excelsior*, which appeared after the research for this study had been completed, has, according to its managers, changed its format, content and personnel in order to adjust itself more realistically to the initial plans. It appears that the principal obstacle to be overcome is the slow acquisition of advertising.

The rise in production costs for all the media, whether printed or electronic, clearly affects the supply of information, the amount of advertising and other factors. Those who are responsible are taking steps in the commercial and tax fields to lighten the new burden but they predict still greater limitations on the quantity of information and its presentation.

Finally, amongst those responsible at both the private and the governmental level, there are signs of a greater understanding of the role of the mass media and of the need to formulate policies at various levels.

Appendix

Socio-economic and cultural data[1]

Area: 50,900 square kilometres or 19,653 square miles.
Population: 1974 estimate, 1,940,000; projection for 1980, 2,323,000.
  Density: 37 inhabitants per square kilometre, or 95 inhabitants per square mile.
  Net immigration: 1972, 1,331, difference between 285,546 emigrants and 286,877 immigrants. Internal migration 0.7 per cent of total population.
  Population distribution: in the Central Plateau: 45 to 55 per cent of the population, approximately 440,000; San José, the capital, population 215,500 (centre of the city); rural population 59 per cent, urban 41 per cent: 14 cities with more than 20,000 inhabitants, or 22.5 per cent; 26 cities with more than 10,000 inhabitants, or 18.8 per cent; 58 cities with more than 5,000 inhabitants, or 21.7 per cent; 255 towns with more than 1,000 inhabitants, or 35.7 per cent; 64 towns with less than 1,000 inhabitants, or 1.3 per cent.
Rate of population growth, 1960–74: an average of 3.1 per cent; rate of growth increase in 1974–75, 2.7 per cent; projection for decade 1973–83, 2.5 per cent.
Age pyramid: from 0 to 4 years, 300,000; 5 to 9 years, 275,000; 10 to 14 years, 273,000; 15 to 19 years, 240,000; 0 to 14 years, 48.2 per cent of the population; 15 to 64 years, 49 per cent of the population; 65 years, 2.8 per cent of the population.
Economically passive population (dependent): 51 per cent; economically active population (productive): 49 per cent.
Labour force, total: 607,000 persons; employed: 564,000; unemployed: 43,000 or 7.1 per cent.
Projection for the decade 1973–82: 285,000 additional workers.
School enrolment: number enrolled from Grades 1 to 12 (1975), 490,000: pre-primary, 13,088; secondary I and II cycles, 380,000.
  Percentage of school-age population enrolled: pre-primary, 22.4 per cent; primary, 90 per cent (half complete the course); secondary, 36 per cent (one-third complete the course); specialized education (vocational), estimated 100,000; higher education, 25,000.

1. For sources, see footnotes throughout the text.

Appendix

Urban literacy, 90 per cent; rural literacy, 86 per cent.
Religious groups: Catholics 90 per cent, Protestants 8 per cent, others 2 per cent.
Economic indices:
  Gross National Product (GNP) (1973 market prices), $1,212 million.
  Average annual income *per capita*, $645.3.
  Over-all annual growth, 1960–73, 6.3 per cent; *per capita*, 3 per cent.
  Origin of GNP 1973 in percentages by sector and employment of the population: agriculture and stock-raising (49 per cent of population), 23 per cent; industries (12 per cent of population), 16 per cent; services and government (39 per cent of population), 61 per cent.
  (Government revenues, 14 per cent of GNP.)
  Distribution of wealth (1972): lowest sector (20 per cent of population), 5.4 per cent of national income; middle sector (60 per cent of population), 44 per cent of national income; upper middle sector (10 per cent of population), 16.2 per cent of national income; high sector (10 per cent of population), 34.4 per cent of national income.
  Motor-cars per 1,000 persons, 25; commercial vehicles, 15 per 1,000 persons.
  Electricity consumption, kilowatt, *per capita*, 1972, 54 kilowatts.
Vital data:
  Life expectancy at birth (1972) for men and women: 69.4 years.
  Daily consumption of proteins, 98 per cent of requirements average.
  Poor or middle low sector, first degree malnutrition 48 per cent, second degree 19 per cent (children 1 to 5 years, first degree 43 per cent, second degree 12.2 per cent, third degree 1.5 per cent).
  Mortality: adults, 5.9 per 1,000 infants, 24 per 1,000.
  Doctors per 100,000 inhabitants (1973), 60.
  Nurses per 100,000 inhabitants (1973), 43.
Communications:
  Telephones: 30 per 1,000 inhabitants (60,000 units).
  Radio receivers: 60 per 1,000 inhabitants (125,000 units), 85 per cent of households in the Central Plateau have a radio.
  Television sets: 40 per 1,000 inhabitants (colour, 1,500 units; black and white, 80,000).
Press, publications and printed matter, stationery, etc. total industry, 100 percentage: publishing (periodicals, books, pamphlets, magazines) 11.7 per cent; personnel: 250 journalists, 850 technicians and allied workers.
  Import of magazines (light reading), estimation: $1 million per year.
  Export, very few magazines. Editorial Costa Rica, 5 per cent of production (30 per cent of this quantity to Central America).
  Annual consumption of newsprint per inhabitant, 4.5 kilograms.
  Internal demand for printed material, percentage of industry, 0.7 per cent.
  Projected growth for four years, 11.3 per cent.
  Circulation of periodicals, daily newspapers: 60 per 1,000 inhabitants

(average) (higher in the Central Plateau, less in remote areas); weekly newspapers: 150 per 1,000 inhabitants.

Books: publishers 3, cumulatively 250 copies per 1,000 inhabitants.

Books and pamphlets published in 1968 (last available figure): 284 (150 social sciences, 42 literature, 92 others).

In fifteen years (up to 1974) Editorial Costa Rica: 200 titles with a total of 600,000 copies.

Public and specialized libraries open to the public, 11 (there are many private libraries); total number of volumes (estimate): 3 million (2.9 million in 1970).

Cinema: total number of cinematograph theatres (1972): 150.

Television: 4 channels, total audience 51.5; channel 6, 26.6; channel 7, 20.3; channel 4, 9.6; channel 11, 1.1 (being reorganized).

Radio: 48 radio broadcasting stations, total audience 33.0.

Principal stations and audiences in metropolitan area: Radio Reloj, 5.8; Radio Columbia, 4.2; Radio Centro, 2.7; Radio Monumental, 2.3; Radio Mil, 2.0; Eco, 2.0; Omega, 1.8; Titania, 1.8; foreign stations reception, 0.1.

Note: There are no adequate studies of total hours on the air for radio or television stations or of advertising budgets and revenues or breakdown of programmes by types (light entertainment, cultural news).

Except when the year is mentioned, the statistics given are from data published from 1970 to 1974 by various sources.

[B.16] CC.76/XX.8/A